The Literature of Food
ALIMENTUM

ISSUE TWO   SUMMER   2006

PUBLISHER
Paulette Licitra

EDITORS
Paulette Licitra
Peter Selgin

POETRY EDITOR
Cortney Davis

DESIGN
Claudia Carlson
Peter Selgin

PUBLICITY DESIGN
Claudia Carlson
Tim Maxwell

WEB DESIGNER
Leigh Wood

EDITORIAL ASSISTANTS
Diana Pittet
Lydia Ross

SPECIAL THANKS TO
Jim Marchese, Mary Lamont,
Marion Niedkowski, Esther Cohen,
Peter Odabashian, Joan Lufrano,
Pinuccia Selgin, Micol Negrin,
Costas Mouzouras & Gotham Wines

ALIMENTUM SPONSORS
The French Culinary Institute, NYC
Sub-Zero & Wolf, Goldman Associates

ALIMENTUM ADVISORY BOARD
Mark Kurlansky, Micol Negrin,
Bonnie Slotnick, Polly Talbot,
Clifford A. Wright

Alimentum is published
twice yearly Winter & Summer

SUBSCRIPTIONS
$18 per year
Please add $6 for Canadian
and foreign subscriptions.
Single copies $10.

Make checks payable to

ALIMENTUM
P.O. Box 776,
New York, NY 10163

DISTRIBUTED BY
Ingram Periodicals
Ubiquity Distributors
Bernhard DeBoer, Inc.

SUBMISSIONS
Manuscripts are read year round.
Please see website for details.

www.alimentumjournal.com

EMAIL INQUIRES TO
editor@alimentumjournal.com

© 2006 BY ALIMENTUM
ALL RIGHTS RESERVED

ISBN # 0-9773528-1-1

Contents

PUBLISHER'S PREFACE	/ 5

FICTION

Nourishment—Michael Onofrey	/ 7
The Baker—Amy Halloran	/ 25
Following the Recipe—Sue Taylor	/ 40
A Brief History of Toast—Angus Woodward	/ 44
Dream of a Rarebit Fiend—Donald Newlove	/ 69
How Birds Taught People to Make Coffee—Margarita Engle	/ 77

POETRY

Three Poems—T.M. De Vos	/ 13
Kitchens are for Cooking—Kerry Trautman	/ 17
Almost Utopia—Gary J. Whitehead	/ 23
The Butter, the Bottle, the Sugar Bowl—Michele Battiste	/ 37
Breakfast—Will Walker	/ 50
Two Poems—Elisa Albo	/ 54
Cheap Food—Susie Paul	/ 57
Thirteen Ways of Looking at a Nantucket Bay Scallop—Annie Kay	/ 67
Shad Chant—Lawrence F. O'Brien	/ 68
Coffee—Jehanne Dubrow	/ 73
Conversation with Neruda—Persis M. Karim	/ 84
Three Meals—Peter Selgin	/ 86
The Twelve-Course Dinner of Regret—Terri Brandmueller	/ 94
Tomato Garden—Kerry Trautman	/ 109
Recipe for Tomato Cabal—Angus Woodward	/ 110
Bartlett—Jamie Granger	/ 114
Let's Go Hog-Wild with Our Peaches—Anthony Russell White	/ 115
Escape From the Fat Farm—Sandy McIntosh	/ 116

Nonfiction

First Growth—Sophie Helene Menin	/ 19
A Writer Makes Cookies—Patsy Anne Bickerstaff	/ 38
Skimming Off the Top—Barbara Cunliffe Singleton	/ 46
Comfort Food—Ann Hood	/ 51
Alphabet Soup Kitchen—Ruth E. Dickey	/ 59
Drinking Lattes in Krakow—Ellen Herbert	/ 75
How to Eat a Pet—Lynn Levin	/ 87
What We Bring to the Table—Margaret MacInnis	/ 96
Tomato Love—C. Kevin Smith	/ 107
Pears—Reamy Jansen	/ 112

Interview

Joanne Harris / 78

Cover Art

Peter Selgin *www.peterselgin.com*

Illustrations

Louis Dunn *www.louisdunn.com*

Publisher's Preface

Summer's here, bringing memories of outdoor food and brilliant hot-weather moments in our lives.

Like the time I first met my husband's cousin, Bianca. She drove us in her *cinquecento* from the Genoa train station to her villa high above the Mediterranean overlooking Portofino. In her lush backyard garden, shaded by a huge laurel tree and an arbor of kiwi fruit, she served us *trenette* with pesto.

Then, food and family drama collided (as they often do in Italy). First, I noted with delight that Bianca's pesto hadn't been made with a food processor, or even ground with a mortar and pestle, but hand-diced to perfect consistency, with tiny squares of basil clinging to the pasta. A moment later came Bianca's shocked expression when we told her we'd be staying for three weeks.

Outdoor feasts are no strangers to literature. There's the Box Hill picnic in Jane Austen's *Emma*, the emotional heart of that story. In Forster's *A Room with a View*, the romance between George and Lucy ignites at a picnic. And in Giuseppe di Lampedusa's *Il Gattopardo* (The Leopard), the Prince fights to maintain his slipping power at an elaborate outdoor feast.

For me, though, one literary picnic stands high above the others, drawn deep from childhood memory:

> *For ev'ry bear that ever there was*
> *Will gather there for certain, because*
> *Today's the day the teddy bears have their picnic…*

So go the lyrics to "The Teddy Bears Picnic," a happy (if slightly foreboding) song—and the blueprint, for me at least, for summer gatherings of hearts and food.

Think of this second issue of *Alimentum* as a picnic basket of literary goodies. Bring it to your favorite outdoor spot—a sidewalk cafe, or a blanket on the beach, or the spot of shade under your favorite tree. Or to a quiet patio table at dusk, when it's just you and the crickets chirping, to digest with a batch of warm cookies and milk—or a snifter of brandy.

Wherever you take it—and wherever it takes you—I hope you'll savor every morsel, feel deeply sated, and then come back for more.

—Paulette Licitra

The fine arts are five in number, namely: painting, sculpture, poetry, music, and architecture, the principal branch of the latter being pastry.
—Antonin Carême

Nourishment

by MICHAEL ONOFREY

Jimmy Smith enters the town in pursuit of food. It is a little after one in the afternoon and it is hot and humid and he is on a bicycle. He is in southern India and he has been traveling in the state of Karnataka since leaving Goa.

He spent the previous night in Shimoga in a cheap hotel. This morning he left Shimoga at seven after having tea, bread and potato *bhaji* in a cafe. With any luck he'll reach Mysore in two or three days.

Jimmy's hungry and he needs food. He can feel it in his stomach, legs, and mind, energy depleted, focus fuzzy, shirt soaked with sweat. It is for food that he stops in this small town instead of pedaling through, for even at a glance he can tell that it has little to offer—a single paved street, which is the road he's on, a few shops, almost all of which have closed for the afternoon.

He dismounts and walks his bicycle along the street, a heavy black bicycle that he bought in Delhi six months before. He's rangy but his body has turned stringy. He looks like a rubber band. He's wearing sunglasses, khaki shorts, sandals and a cotton shirt with a floral design. On his head there's a baseball cap, which is really a football cap, since the logo above the bill advertises the Oakland Raiders.

A slinking dog garners Jimmy's attention. The animal is across the street and is moving sideways, fur blotted, ribs prominent, eyes drizzling. Jimmy keeps the dog in view. There is no traffic. The town is quiet, a parked tractor, a parked truck. Jimmy is on a lesser route and purposely so, Mangalore and Bangalore attracting most of the traffic, Jimmy's direction is between the two, immediate destination: Mysore. Beyond Mysore he'll continue south until he crosses the Palk Strait on a ferry to begin pedaling in Sri Lanka.

Jimmy sees an open doorway to his right. There is no sign. There is only an opened plank door on a whitewashed single-story structure. He can't say why, but he senses food. He pushes his bicycle off the paved road, edge of the road broken as if chewed. Between the road and the buildings along this street there is a swath of dirt. Jimmy brings his bicycle up on its heavy rear stand in front of the open doorway but leaves enough space for people to enter. He locks the bike with a chain that he's taken from a wicker basket attached to the handlebars of his bicycle. But more importantly, he has positioned the bike so he can see it from inside the shop, if indeed it is a shop that he has decided to enter.

Jimmy takes a cloth shoulder bag from the basket of his bike and takes his cap off and puts it in the basket. He takes his sunglasses off and puts them in his shoulder bag and loops the strap of the bag over his shoulder. He steps over a threshold, which is a piece of wood similar to a four-by-four, top of the wood rounded and worn.

The floor of the room he has entered is dirt, but unlike outside the dirt is damp and packed hard and it has a slightly reddish tint, where outside the dirt is dry and chalky. Since having left the lowlands of the coast with its thick vegetation the land has been relatively flat and dry, thorny bush, pebbled surface; but there have been exceptions: Linganamakki Reservoir, Tunga River. Before reaching Mysore he will weave through low hills that are home to a large sandalwood forest, to which certain industries in Mysore owe their existence: fragrant oil, incense, and aromatic wooden carvings and boxes. But now the damp floor and the shadowed room are a respite from the heat and the sun that has been at him since seven this morning.

His eyes adjust and he sees there are half a dozen wooden tables with low stools in the room, seats of the stools braided straw, wood of the tables unfinished. There is no one in the room, not a single person. A square hole high up on the wall to his right and then another on the wall to his left allow shafts of light to illuminate the room irregularly as does the open doorway. There is also another hole just over a low sink on the rear wall.

Jimmy yells hello and stands and waits. After a moment a heavyset man emerges from behind a curtain on the rear wall. The man wears a white *lungi* that is slightly soiled. His feet are bare and so is his torso. A string over his shoulder loops diagonally down the front and back of the man's body to where it completes a circle at the man's ample waist. On the man's forehead, above his nose and above a pair of thick, black-framed glasses, is a smudge of beige paste. The man doesn't say anything. He just moves further to his left where he busies himself in a dark corner.

Someone steps through the doorway in back of Jimmy. Jimmy turns and sees a middle-aged man in a pair of dirty plaid trousers and a striped short-sleeved shirt. The man walks to the sink and bends and turns on the faucet and rinses his hands under a weak flow of water. He turns the faucet off and shakes water from his hands as he walks to a table and sits down.

Following the man's example, Jimmy goes to the sink and rinses his hands and flicks drops of water onto the dirt floor and walks to a table and sits down. The man in the red-green-and-white-striped shirt is to Jimmy's left. There is one table between them. Jimmy can see his bicycle from where he sits. He puts his shoulder bag on the stool next to him to his right. His real valuables of course are in a money belt around his waist inside his shorts and underwear and next to his skin.

The man in the *lungi* places a glass of water on the striped-shirt man's table and places a glass of water on Jimmy's table. The man in the *lungi* returns to the dark corner and fetches two banana leaves. One leaf goes on the table before the man to Jimmy's left, the other leaf goes on Jimmy's table. The ends of the leaves are cut off so that each leaf forms a large rectangle. Jimmy looks up at the man in the *lungi* who has just set the leaf on his table and says *bhaji*. The man wags his big head, stubble on his fleshy jowls, stubble over the dome of his skull, stubble gray and black. The man walks away. Jimmy knows that a wagging head in India could mean any number of things. In this case, the man is saying no *bhaji*.

The man to Jimmy's left picks up his glass of water and pours a little water on his banana leaf. He sets the glass down and begins pushing the water around the leaf with his fingers. Satisfied that the entire leaf is wet he picks it up by the edge and gives it a good shake over the floor. The leaf goes back onto the table. Jimmy, having gotten the idea, does the same. But Jimmy knows that the water is going to do nothing for the banana leaf in terms of hygiene, for it's the water in India that poses a major health risk. But Jimmy is hungry and as far as he can tell there are no other choices in this small town, which isn't even on his map. Jimmy regrets not having looked for peanuts in Shimoga.

The man in the *lungi* comes out of the dark corner with a pail of white rice. He spoons a large helping onto one side of the banana leaf at the striped-shirt man's table, then comes to Jimmy's table and does the same. He returns to the dark corner. After a moment he materializes carrying an aluminum tray with six tin cups. From each cup the man spoons a blotch of soupy mixture onto the banana leaf at the striped-shirt man's table. He leaves space between each blotch so the puddles don't mix. Also, these watery helpings don't edge up against the rice. The man in the *lungi* comes to Jimmy's table and deposits six dollops of saucy vegetables on one side of Jimmy's banana leaf, then returns to his dark corner. A moment later, Jimmy sees the man is sitting on a chair at the edge of the darkness of the corner, smoking a *bidi*.

Meanwhile the man to Jimmy's left has picked up a clot of rice with the fingers of his right hand and has dipped the rice in one of the soupy pools and brought the damp rice to his mouth and shoved it into his mouth with his fingers, a deft, practiced motion. The man chews.

Jimmy follows the man's example but is careful when dabbing the rice in one of the soupy splotches. He starts with the puddle to the left intending to proceed from left to right as if he were reading. In each of the soupy pools bits of vegetable are visible but not recognizable. They are cut very small, pale greens mostly.

The first sample goes into Jimmy's mouth and it is hot—hot, hot, hot—spicy hot. Jimmy can't detect any flavor other than fire. He puts a wad of dry rice into his mouth in an attempt to neutralize the spice. The glass of water on his table is tempting, but Jimmy does not dare to touch it. He's been sick a number of times—stomach, intestines, diarrhea. He thinks about the bottle of Pepsi in the basket of his bicycle. He decides to try the second puddle of runny vegetables, hoping for a neutral flavor, or better yet a sweet vegetable flavor. But the second mixture proves to be the same as the first—only hot. Jimmy stuffs more plain rice into his mouth and wonders if all six sauces are the same. Their colors are slightly different and so are their textures, but between the first two samplings there is no difference in taste. Jimmy begins to hiccup.

The man to Jimmy's left seems to be enjoying his meal. He chews with relish, mouth moving vigorously. The man in the *lungi* approaches the middle-aged man's table with the tray of assorted dips and replenishes the man's banana leaf.

The *lungi* man glances at Jimmy's leaf, but second helpings are obviously not needed. Jimmy hiccups periodically and he sweats across his forehead. The man in the *lungi* returns to his dark corner and after a moment sits down on the chair at the edge of the darkness. He is no longer smoking. He only sits looking at the doorway with a view of the street. The man to Jimmy's left digs in anew.

Jimmy has worked his way through five of the six vegetable sauces. He now tries the last pool, which turns out to be the same as the others, just plain hot—hot in his mouth, hot in his throat, hot in his stomach. From then on he eats only unflavored white rice.

The man to Jimmy's left sits back on his stool. His food is gone and he seems satisfied. After a moment, he folds his banana leaf up to form a pouch. He picks this up with one hand and stands and takes the leaf to the sink. Jimmy turns and watches. The man puts the banana leaf through the hole above the sink. A cow's face appears at the hole. With its tongue the cow picks up the banana leaf from where it lies on a short chute made of concrete or adobe. The man washes his hands while the cow chews. The man walks away from the sink and shakes his hands out over the dirt floor. The man in the *lungi* stands and approaches. The man who has eaten pays for his meal and goes out the door of the shop and disappears.

Jimmy folds his banana leaf up and takes it to the hole in the wall above the sink. The cow is there. Jimmy can see it outside, waiting. He puts the leaf on the chute and the cow comes forward and picks it up with its tongue. The cow is white with brown spots and it is slim. The cow's face looks remarkably human, eyes almond-shaped. Jimmy washes his hands and shakes them out over the floor. He picks up his shoulder bag. The man in the *lungi* comes forward and states a price. It is cheap. Jimmy pays the man and leaves the shop.

Jimmy unlocks his bicycle, puts his cap on, and puts his shoulder bag in the basket of his bike, foregoing his sunglasses. His stomach is crawling, but he no longer sweats or hiccups. He hopes he doesn't get sick. A car blasts its horn and races through the town. Jimmy watches it disappear into the distance. Jimmy turns and looks at the town as it bakes beneath a midday sun—nothing stirs. The tractor and truck are still parked but the dog is gone.

Jimmy mounts his bike and begins pedaling. But for his twisting stomach he feels better. He has gained some energy.

The simple buildings of the town thin quickly and then cease altogether. Up ahead on Jimmy's left there is a large tree. His gray eyes focus on the tree; something about it invites curiosity. In the shade of the tree an old woman sits on a square of cloth, stones weighing the cloth down at the corners. Before her is a pile of bananas. Jimmy coasts across the road and glides up to the woman and stops. The woman watches him, her eyes moist, her complexion dark and deeply creased. A bead of saliva glistens along her lower lip. She wears a simple brown sari of fabric more functional than decorative, more course than delicate, more of the earth than ethereal. She is barefoot. There are bangles on her arms. Her arms are skinny but sinewy with muscle.

Jimmy pulls his bicycle up onto its stand. He takes some money from a change purse he keeps in his shoulder bag. He hands some coins to the woman, who extends her shriveled hand to accept them. His fingers brush against the woman's palm. Her palm is like leather. She holds the currency under her eyes and looks at it. She drops the coins on the cloth, picks up a large bunch of bananas and holds them aloft for him to take. He takes the bananas from her and puts them in the basket of his bicycle. He says thank you and the woman nods. Jimmy pedals away as the woman watches him. After a while he looks back. She is still watching him.

Scrub vegetation fills the landscape. Errant crows caw from out of a hot sky. The transaction with the woman has left Jimmy in a quiet, peaceful mood. He doesn't feel the heat so much. There is now rhythm to his pedaling as opposed to sheer labor. He pulls over onto the dirt shoulder and straddles his bike. There are twelve bananas in the bunch. Each six inches in length and fat. He snaps one off, peels it and eats it. Bananas are safe—no washing, no cutting. They are sweet and they settle the stomach. Jimmy tosses the peel away and instantly a crow swoops down to retrieve it. As the bird flies off with its prize, another crow wheels and tries to steal it. Jimmy eats a second banana and tosses the peel. Birds fight over it.

Jimmy starts pedaling. Short stocky trees begin to appear. A smear of vapor colors the horizon. The day's heat has begun to abate. A green cloud turns in the distance, advancing upon him. He stops in the road and straddles his bicycle to watch. A flock of small green parrots, their numbers vast, pass low overhead. He looks up, wing-beats and squawking in his ears.

Three Poems
by T.M. De Vos

Pumpkin

A boy grew a seed,
cleared a ring for it from the grass.
He poured milk on the puncture,
warm as the liquid he'd leave
in his own hand, soon.

The vines tangled out of the soil,
and he shook them like reins,
looking for flowers.
When the fruit burst through its bud,
he pumped it in his hand,
checking for prints
from whatever might have touched it.
As it grew, he weighed it on his lap,
its round bottom cool on his thighs.

He dug around the stem,
thinking of the poem
about the man who puts his wife away;
imagining he'd see her head
as he pulled off the lid
and stared into the fruit-brain,
a wig sewn with buttons.

Apple

A girl threw apples to a boy,
careful not to nick them on the fence,
the stretched knit of the wire.
She brought him a big green one
she had sketched in class,
shading the fibers of its peel,
the threads gripping each other like purls in a scarf.

In the winter, she forgot him
the way you forget a stray dog you find, and feed—
how do you trace where you have sent it,
your food still warm in its belly?

Years later, in the city,
she was young and drunk, sharing a cab
with a man from her same province.
That someone I loved could be dead.
That he probably is, she repeated.

He pressed her cheek as if it were the skin of a fruit
he had just decided he wanted.
There were numbers on his arm
where the boy's would have been.
He rolled the consonants in his mouth like hard lozenges:
I remember you, your yellow braids.

She lay under his blanket,
watching him toss a russet apple
into the air above their faces.
Under that wrist, the boy's,
like a branch grown over wire.

Lightness

In a moment of crisis we can betray anything.
The trapped body drops radii
easily as man plants himself in woman
or a crab sacrifices a leg.

I was light with someone, once,
wanted him to weigh on me
the way apples deform bread.
But there was only lack, the lifting of his imprint
from me, then nothing—dust, atmosphere,
other dimensions blowing through my chest.

I cannot believe, as Sartre did,
that there is only the *fait accompli*,
the completed act—

Wistfulness is its own force,
the bruise-dent of lack has a gravity,
a power to attract matter,
fractionally; negative exponents
were created for this energy

and that of my mother, up early,
cracking eggs onto chaos, our only placemats
joining our chairs in congruent legs;
flipping her failed pancakes—

This is what I have for you,
imperfect and heavy—

too dark, thicker than the plates—*like manhole covers,*
I had said—

Alimentum

She poured batch after batch,
dishing me their book-weights
until I took the bowl from her,
and with my steady hands
poured a circle—perfect,
free of pseudopods—
and lifted it,
clean as the sole of a new shoe.

Kitchens are for Cooking
by Kerry Trautman

"I didn't want the baby,"

she told me, waiting for
the hollandaise to foam.
I watched her arms reach for the whisk.

"So I went to Toronto with the old painter.
He had a spare room."

She minced four cloves of garlic,
finely, by hand.
I heard rain.

"There was a full bottle of whiskey
on the nightstand each morning.
Till I lost the baby, and still after."

She crumbled some feta
on a salad of kale and dried cranberries.
I memorized the red of the berries.

"He started coming in my room at night.
I'd pretend to stay asleep."

She buttered her Calphalon pan.
It sizzled and smoked orange.
I thought about sunsets.

"It was good whiskey."

She checked the portabellos in the oven,
heat wafted over us, and purple light.
I let the heat in through my teeth.

"After I came home,
I moved from whiskey to wine."

I dipped my finger in the hollandaise,
she wanted me to taste it.

"We need cheddar,"

she said, pouring two plastic cups
full of zinfandel,

"sharp, sharp cheddar."

First Growth: An Essay on Love & Wine

by Sophie Helene Menin

Some women marry older men for wealth, some for security, some for real estate. Mine was a love marriage, but had it not been, I might have married Geoffrey for the wine. A man who has been collecting wine for decades comes with the most sublime baggage. His cellar yields cases of treasures that tantalize the palate, reveal the past and encourage one to rejoice in the present. Each bottle bears 750 ml of story: European vacations; treasures to mark special occasions; gifts from ex-girlfriends; the singular bottle from the small estate discovered at an out-of-the-way wine store; barter from clients who could not pay their bills; the big splurge.

Wine and matrimony are closely linked for us. We registered at Sherry-Lehmann. We even purchased a bottle of vintage Le Montrachet, the ultimate white Burgundy, to sip when we took our vows. At the last minute my husband decided it would be sacrilegious to open such a bottle without the proper time to linger and instead poured the Matanzas Creek, a fine quality California Chardonnay we had chosen to serve two hundred guests. The wedding video reveals a surprised pucker across my face as my lips touch the silver chalice.

Last summer we catalogued the collection. Geoffrey pulled bottles from the cav and I took notes. We sorted the list by region, winemaker and vintage. Then we evaluated each bottle to determine whether we should store the wine at home or let it age in our locker. About halfway through the process I became giddy.

I knew I had married into wine, but I did not know I had the auspicious luck of wedding just as a large chunk of the collection had entered into the "not getting any better" stage. Scores of bottles had reached their prime and basked in it long enough to demand immediate attention. Since then we have been opening distinctive bottles as if every Saturday night was New Year's Eve. Either I cook and my husband searches for the meal's perfect mate, or he declares which wine we shall try and together we design a menu to set it off in the most favorable light.

I tend to like imperfect wines the best, like that one bottle of 1982 Chateau Ducru-Beaucaillou that had turned, just a little. This classic St. Julien, born on 120 acres of gravelly hills overlooking France's Gironde River, should have possessed a deep claret color. When we drank it, flames of orange sparked against the edge of the hand-blown crystal glass. The orange signaled decay, but you could still taste the nuanced undertones of cedar, cassis and ripe blackberries in this slightly unraveled beauty and imagine the wine in its prime. The Ducru-Beaucaillou reminded me of so many women I love and admire. Aging enchanters with great bone structure and even greater depth, who no longer posses the rosy glow of youth, yet remain objects of wonder.

I also appreciate the wines we opened too young, like the 1999 Mondavi Reserve Cabernet Sauvignon. One cannot drink this wine simply by uncorking the bottle. It took hours for the protective coil, a tightly bound double helix of tannins and alcohol, to unwind and reveal hints of how, if stored properly, it will mature over time. We had to be patient, take detours, drink a lesser wine as an intermezzo, before we could experience the lush tapestry of dark fruit, licorice and exotic spices. I didn't mind. How often do you have the chance to taste the future? We have a dozen more.

The cellar contains quirky wines too. A Schwarz Riesling from Germany, Buffalo Blood from a friend's ranch in Marin, Bull's Blood from Hungary. Then there are the perfect wines. These are the ones I am just coming to understand. I seem to lack an intuitive affinity for perfection. It's easier to appreciate imperfection. It grabs your attention. You can't escape it. Imperfection is human; perfection smacks of the divine.

Recently my husband decided to celebrate the third anniversary of our engagement by opening what might be the best bottle of wine in our collection, a 1961 Lafite Rothschild. His sister gave him the bottle twenty-five years ago.

Lafite Rothschild is one of five Bordeaux wines that earned the designation first growth under the Classification of 1855, one of six if you include the sauterne Château d'Yquem. Most wine aficionados consider 1961 to be the region's premier mid-20th century vintage.

I must admit at first I was a little disappointed by the choice. I had wanted to roast a duck. I had a vision of crisp skin, dark fatty meat and a 1985 Shafer helping to restore the much-maligned reputation of Merlot. He knew my fantasy. I had articulated it on more than one occasion. Still, he said Lafite Rothschild was not a wine for duck. Lamb or veal would make a better match. How could I complain?

Wanting to be an equal partner to this grand bottle, I rummaged through my books and asked my friends what to make. In *The Slow Mediterranean Kitchen*, Paula Wolfert suggested veal shanks smothered in carrots, chestnuts and chanterelles, a favorite recipe of her daughter, who works as a wine importer. The recipe took three hours to prepare. I seared meat, rendered lardons, caramelized onions, braised and basted. Finally, I plated the veal shanks in a large earthenware dish over steaming spaetzle. There was enough food for six.

As the earthy aromas perfumed our home, we set the table, lit a fire and opened the night's main act. We were dressed casually in jeans, bare feet, and comfortable tees. Still, dinner held all the promise and anxious expectation of a lavish black-tie affair.

Geoffrey pulled out my chair before I sat down, then walked to the credenza and poured a small amount of wine from the decanter into a tasting glass to inspect. He returned to the table holding a white towel beneath the decanter's rim and poured the Lafite into our hand-blown crystal goblets. After he sat down, we raised our glasses and toasted to our life together. We sipped and savored. A 1961 Lafite Rothschild represents silky elusive perfection. Light on the tongue and supremely balanced with subtle hints of almonds and violets, the symmetry brings to mind the elegance of a Bach fugue.

Moments later I bit into the veal shank. The chestnuts, lardons and braised veal bespoke essays in lusty indulgence for carnivorous appetites. I had set out silver caviar spoons to scoop the marrow, which I adore. As I dipped the curved blade into the soft fat, the scraping of the spoon against the bone brought to mind my bulldog Satchmo and how she would relish this meal. At that moment, I realized I had miss-stepped. The luscious veal shanks seemed somehow immodest in the presence of such a noble wine.

Gazing across the candlelight at my husband, I could tell that he too recognized the imbalance. We both chose to be polite, to respect the integrity of all the delights that graced our table, even if they were not complementary. We chewed our food slowly, savoring each morsel, then took a breath to cleanse our palates before sipping.

On this third anniversary of our engagement, fine food and drink encouraged us to make space for difference, to value both finesse and lust. Of course, a tender rack of lamb would have been a more elegant mate for the heavenly first growth and a bold Barolo could have stared down the haute-peasant cuisine more fully (it did so splendidly the next night). Hopefully, like dancing together, we'll have years to get these pairings right.

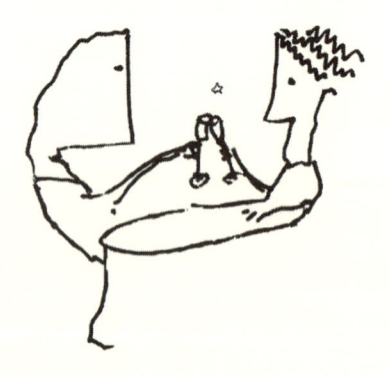

Almost Utopia
by Gary J. Whitehead

If I could cook for her—
    roasted lamb with a demiglace,
        say, or coq au vin

(anything with wine),
    potatoes baked in their dirty skins—
        while her wet clothes

dripped on the line
    and Allen's hummingbirds
        dipped at the sugared water

hung above the deck; and if the light
    was just right, and the breeze
        easy, carrying a dry trace

of bay and the madrones'
    yellow leaves; if she liked
        fresh-ground pepper,

the sound of it cracking
    in the mill, and sea salt, too,
        and coffee sentenced

to the antique oubliette of the hand-
    cranked grinder; our laughter lost
        for a time in the teapot's whistle,

then—what? Who would I be
    for her or for me but the man
        who in the undreamt world

tires too soon of talk
    and can't stand a cluttered table.
        In the middle of some story

told more to fill the empty space
    between our plates than to reveal
        anything meaningful,

I'd find myself dreaming
    of the green river, of the way
        it hugs my legs when I wade in it,

or of the lizard I saw
    doing push-ups on my steps.
        But I'd be looking in her eyes,

wet and brown, and thinking
    at the same time that this
        is what love is—the sweet,

burnt crust of crème brûlée
    and the dark hair that keeps
        falling across her pretty face.

The Baker
by Amy Halloran

I am a mother but I'm not much of a baker. In a country where M-O-M spells apple pie, this is tough. I've tried to learn how to make cakes, but recipes don't work like equations for me. When I try to use mixes, the results taste and look like the boxes they came in, cardboard and flat.

If I can't bake how can I be a good mother? This question wakes me earlier and earlier every morning and instead of tossing and turning, I walk away from the house as if I will leave for good, but I know that my feet are on a leash that will lead me home.

I walk past the market where grocers are hurling boxes of fruit into the back of the store. I pass the barbershop. The colored swirls on its pole are still, but the bakery on the next block shines. Each night I am drawn like a bug to this light, and I try to imagine myself inside of it, baking. The perfume of yeast spilling from its open windows is sweet as incense, calling me to this altar of sugar.

One morning my devotion is interrupted by a truck filling up with baked goods and blocking the sidewalk. I don't want to risk getting hit by a tired driver, so I wait and notice a foam of frosting spilling from a trash can.

Lifting the lid, I swipe my finger through the cake and taste. It's good, not old or moldy. Two other cans are filled with cake, too, so I find a cardboard round and a square box and pile pieces in a mound to take home. I will make my family a cake.

While my husband and son get ready to leave the house, I shape the cake and mix mud colors of frosting in the pantry with the door shut. The cake looks better than my best efforts, and stands triumphant on a crystal pedestal in the middle of the kitchen table.

Petey and Gary ignore the cake while they eat breakfast. I make sandwiches and hum to the commercials on the radio. When I take the cake to the counter, Gary and Petey stop chewing, notice their stopping, and start again. They try not to watch me wrap two pieces in waxed paper. My husband clears his throat.

"Mom," says my son, who never asks for anything.

"Yes?"

"Can I have more cereal?"

"Of course," I say. I know he wanted to ask about the cake.

Petey gets up to get a new cereal box but I push his shoulder down, and go to the pantry myself. I don't want him to see the remnants of my 'baking.'

At dinner nobody talks about the cake. We don't talk about food because before Gary and I said, "I do," we agreed that our families spent too much time on the topic. Smiling over steaks in a restaurant, we thought that ignoring food in our married life would save us from the limits of our own beginnings. Steering free of the subject, we and the children we made would soar. Gary and Petey excel in all they do but generally I can't find my wings. So you can imagine that I'm flying as I bring out the cake for dessert.

Silently, we eat three slices. The cake and frosting are not in typical shapes, but the taste is fine. I hum over little mouthfuls, happy for my victory. Gary and Petey try to hide their smiles.

When everyone's done my husband and I retire to the living room. Petey carries the cake into the kitchen. I picture him putting the leg of the plate too close to the edge of the counter and, as if my worry necessitates disaster, I hear the whole thing fall.

Petey sucks in his breath as I walk in the kitchen.

"It's okay," I say, but he doesn't believe me. I pick up pieces of glass and cake and put them in the trash. "It's okay, go do your homework. I'll pack the dishwasher."

"No," he says. "I want to."

He scrapes plates and puts them in their slots, pours detergent in the machine and shuts the door, turns it on.

"There," he says. "Now I can do my homework."

I kiss his forehead and finish cleaning the floor. I return to the living room, where I wait for my husband to tell me about his day. Maybe the cake, its presence or its exit, made him forget his ritual unwinding, so I nudge him.

"What?" he says.

"Your day."

"Oh, yes." He lists his day in reverse, from five o'clock back to nine, but he can't bring the day back to life for me. I don't mind because I feel good for the first time in ages, so good that I want to make love. I give him the eye, but we've been here so long, in these chairs with their winged shoulders that we are invisible. I touch his knee.

"Honey," I say. He raises his eyebrows, as if this is an answer. "I want to go upstairs."

"Fine. Then, do."

"I want to go upstairs with you."

"Oh," he says, trying to stop my hand from its turns on his knee. "But Petey is still up."

"Okay," I say, reaching for him, "let's go to the basement."

I lead him down the stairs and he slides a thin bolt behind us. Our basement is divided, like us. I have a sofa and rug, a little black and white TV and some end tables. My son has a ping pong table and shelves for bats and balls. My husband has a workbench, which he organizes on the weekends.

I take Gary to the sofa and force him horizontal. Unzipped, his penis is perpendicular. I kick off my shoes and lift up my skirt. He comes quickly, embarrassed by my desire so I make him help me with his tongue.

Afterwards, I can tell he has questions he won't ask. We go back to the living room and he tells me about his day again. This time, he is a hero.

I sleep better than I have in ages but wake to the sound of music. I take Gary's hand off my hip and sneak out for a walk. Something inside me feels settled, but I figure I might as well get some cake, if there's more to be had.

It is dark-dark and the dogs don't bark at me. There are no trucks at the supermarket, none at the bakery, either, but the naked baker is sweating and shoving cakes in the garbage.

He is a hairy man, and heavy, with a belly like a large loaf of bread.

"I am the baker," he says, inviting me inside.

I am so shocked I don't know what to do but obey. I follow him and he ties on an apron before extending a sticky hand.

"I am Rosemary," I say, and my name feels beautiful in my mouth. It has been a while since I thought of myself as me and not as my son's mother or my husband's wife.

"Getting some exercise?" he asks, smoothing his black curls. Globs of frosting and crumbs of cake stick to his hair. He licks his forearm.

"I woke up," I say. "I heard music."

"Someone singing in your dreams?"

"I don't know," I tell him.

"You're welcome to stay, but I have work to do. Please don't think I'm rude."

"Oh no, go right ahead," I say. He moves smoothly, as if what I see weighs less than it should. His buttocks are firm. I stare at his bare behind while he muscles dough into loaves. I walk around the table so I can look him in the eye.

"Don't they have machines for that?" I ask.

"They have machines for everything. They have machines to help you breathe but you still use your lungs, right?"

I don't answer.

"I am right," he answers. He kneads some more. "So, Rosemary, what do you do besides prowl?"

His smile makes me worry that I still smell of sex.

"I am a mother and a wife," I say. "I am very active in the community."

"Then you must have a husband and children," says the baker.

"A child. Petey. He's eleven."

"A fine woman like you should have more children, Rosemary. Just think of the lonely souls without mothers. Just think of who you are depriving."

"Who am I depriving if no one's born yet?" I say too quickly, and wonder why I'm so intimate with this stranger.

I feel naked. I don't even know his name and I have given him my details. The baker laughs and lifts his arms from the dough.

"Come here," he says. I reach across the table to shove his hands into the dough.

"No," I say, storming to the door.

I walk home fast, remembering the cake I wanted to get only when I open my own door. I take off my shoes and walk upstairs. In the bathroom I wet a washcloth and drape it on my face. What was I doing, walking in the middle of the night? I get in bed and hold my husband. Eventually his alarm rings, a steady string of beeps. He untangles himself from me as he turns off the machine. I curl up and watch him pee. I like how there isn't any flesh to hide him. While he is shaving, his erection bumps the sink. Instead of asking for a preview of his day, I ask to have sex again.

We usually use condoms, but last night and this morning I didn't take the time for safety. As Gary comes inside me again, I wonder what should we do. I don't particularly want another baby, except perhaps because the baker thought I should be a mother again. The baker was disgusting, kneading our bread with his bare hairy hands, standing there with his ass wide open to the world.

All the same, I hold his opinion in some esteem.

I worry all morning about being pregnant, and about the stranger I gave permission to enter my life. No matter what, I know I'll go back to the bakery. I nap in the afternoon, and dream of sharing his kitchen. In my dream we make a wedding cake with a fondant frosting smooth as a skating rink, and put little dolls of my family on top. My husband and son, the real ones, not the dolls, cut the cake together, and smile as they eat. The baker and I stand watching them. My teacher touches me like a father, puts his hand around my shoulder. He is proud of what I've learned. If my husband objects to the touch, he doesn't reveal his envy. He doesn't let on that it is a miracle, teaching me to bake, but the baker knows what he has done, and gooses me on the behind before I follow my family upstairs to put Petey to bed, and take my place beside Gary.

Only my husband isn't there as I wake from my dream with my very real kitchen beneath me. I wish the baker were below me, ready to teach me about food.

I go through the motions of making dinner, but I am already in the night, ready for my baker.

The next thing I know I am in my bed, waking to singing, soft in the distance like a ghost. I walk through the quiet house checking on my family. They are beautiful asleep, suspended between days and obligations. I put on my coat and scarf and follow the voice. Of course it leads me through the neighborhood and past the supermarket, whose neon is blinking OPEN 24 HOURS although it is closed. The singing is coming from the bakery, whose small windowpanes are dirty. I rub a peephole with my finger, but still I can't see.

I rap on the door but the baker can't hear me so I let myself in. The long tables furthest from the ovens are covered with cakes, single layer rounds and crowd-sized sheets, circles stacked for birthdays and trimmed with curly icing. The baker is naked except for a tutu. He is screaming opera, and dancing on his toes, decorating the cakes with a big white tube of frosting. He does a twirl between each cake, holding the tube above his head or in front of his stomach, and he doesn't see me until he gets to the end of the table.

"Hello!" he sings, dropping the frosting and holding out his arms.

This place seems less real than my dream. We stand frozen as I decide whether I can believe where I am.

"You never told me your name," I say finally, "so I don't know how to greet you."

"I've been the baker so long I forgot my own name. What do you think of that?"

He smiles a stretch of red flesh that is both lecherous and endearing. He comes toward me.

I am used to longer arms. The baker's barely meet behind me. I look over his shoulder at the cakes. "Be yours," I read on the first cake, and I consider Gary. My whole married life I never wanted anyone else's affection. Now I am near to a man who isn't my husband, but the proximity isn't the thing that scares me. What frightens me is my alibi.

I know I won't tell my husband about the baker, because to tell my husband about the baker I would have to mention food. Food is crude and taboo, so my marriage is safe. Adultery is easy, I think to myself. It is a piece of cake.

The baker is singing opera, holding me close and whirling me with him, up and down the length of the kitchen from the truck door to the ovens. Maybe, I think, I was mistaken. Maybe the baker only wants to dance.

"Wait," I say. "I want to read the cakes."

The baker is huffing and he puffs out the words even though I can read his flourishy cursive.

"*Be Yours!*" he says. "*Be Yours! Be Mine! Be Ours!* Would you like a piece of cake?" he asks. I nod. He grabs some cake and frosting and puts it in my mouth like we've just been married. I don't want it to be erotic but it is. Still, we don't make love, and I forget to take cake home.

That day, I happen to have an appointment at the gynecologist's. I am armed with birth control when I return to the baker's, drawn by his song. I find a one-man parade of pinks and swirls. He seems to be eternally jolly but from what I read on the cakes I guess that he is awfully sad.

The answer to life is a question?

The sum of your desires equals what you won't get.

Plus he wrecks the cakes he makes. Happy people do not throw tables of cake into the trash. Happy people find other people who like to eat cake. Maybe, I hope, sex will make him happy.

"Rosemary," he says. "I want to fuck you."

I have never used the term before, in reference to the act or anything else. The difference adds to my armor and makes it that much easier to divide my baker from my husband.

I wonder if my baker has had other insomniacs who turned to him for comfort, but it feels like I am the first to make angels in the flour on his tables, on the floor.

The next night, when I sleep with my husband I dream of my baker, dancing and singing. I dream of the bakery hollow without him working, the ovens on and burning flour while he quietly fucks me beside my husband, who sleeps.

As we continue, the baker's inscriptions remain morose. Sex doesn't seem to cheer him up so I bring him books of quotes, Bartlett's, Chairman Mao's. Eventually, he writes phrases from them in royal icing. After we've been together a few months I suggest he consider not wrecking his cakes, and the next day a truck from a food bank pulls up as I am leaving.

Magically, the baker gives me an understanding of the relationship of flour to fat and I begin to bake. My husband and son are pleased with the results. I know because although they cannot congratulate me on any dessert or flavor, conversation at the table suddenly exists. My boys now discuss sports, punctuating their sentences with clean forks raised in the air like fists. They talk about the weather as if it were a close friend.

I tell my baker how I had been a failure in the kitchen until I fucked him, and this makes him want to fuck me more. He turns up the opera and afterward he whispers recipes for buttercream. In the daytime I read cookbooks and the language makes sense.

"Honey," my husband asks one morning, while I am watching him shave. "How did you learn to bake?"

I turn away. I don't care about him carving his face, his day. I get out of bed and put on my robe.

"Have you talked with Petey about the birds and the bees?" I ask.

"No," he says. "But what about learning to bake?"

"Hey," I say, "what about the rule?"

He stares at me, his jaw half clean, and waits for an answer. I won't let down the wall we built.

Despite my resistance our family persists. Petey grows, and Gary goes to work. When the boy goes to college, the house feels only slightly emptier than it has. I delight in the extra room in my life, and stretch my curiosity from dessert into dinner, after discovering the religion of locally grown food.

The baker discovered it first, and converted me. Gone are the nights of cake parades like when I met him; ingredients and products are precious. He now grinds his own flour, and prefers to use grain grown near us in Vermont. He invites me to go with him to France, where he can see special ovens and decide if he should buy one. I decline his generous offer. He threatens to cease seeing me, but I do not change my mind, and he travels without me, bringing home raw milk cheeses he smuggled in his suitcase.

"This is not local," I pretend to protest.

"It was local when I wasn't close to you," the baker says.

I eat the cheese, satisfied that I've kept the compartments of my life distinct.

I see the baker at a farmers' market maybe one day a week. We just sizzle in public, don't talk or touch. Occasionally I travel great distances to purchase cuts from a particular breed of animal. I prepare extra servings and bring them on my nighttime visits, and the baker and I discuss the food, where it comes from, how I made what. He offers suggestions on herbs and spices, on the way I slice certain vegetables.

Sometimes, when I look at the man I married, it seems he might explode.

I can tell that he wants to talk about food. He wants to know why the quality of his meals has so improved, but we stick to the rule. If we break the rule, I am afraid nothing will hold us together.

He's always had chances to discuss food: when we accept dinner invitations, at holiday buffets, and with waiters and waitresses. I love to watch him talk to other people about flavors and textures.

The patterns of our life proceed, as if we are endless spools of thread that will never stop feeding a loom. Baker, lover, wife, mother, husband. My son visits periodically, and dares to try to talk about food.

"Mom," he says, "this sauce is incredible."

I wag my finger and smile, forgiving his rebellion.

"You have to tell me how you made it," he says. "I don't get anything like this at school."

I wag my finger again, and look at his father teasingly. I know the man wants to join the boy in quizzing me, and that is why I give him the smile too, to perish the thought.

"How do you expect me to cook for a girlfriend if you won't give me your recipes?" Petey begs.

"You may look at the books in the kitchen," I say, the most I've ever said of food.

When he does bring home a girl he announces he'd like to marry, she behaves herself at table by not talking about the meal. I am proud of my son. What he and his fiancée choose to do with the subject is their own business, and I am grateful that he respects our boundaries.

The wedding is held in the city park. During the ceremony, I can see the bakery from the gazebo. I keep checking to see when the baker will bring the cake. I am terrified that he won't. He and my husband have never been together. I am worried that the baker will make a scene, or, worse yet, fall on his nerves and dump the cake as he wheels it over the sidewalk and across the street. But the cake arrives flawlessly, at the same time as white-gloved attendants serve hors d'oeuvres.

"This pâté is extraordinary!" a guest says to me.

"What a lovely day!" I say. "How lucky we are it did not rain. Look, the sky is our canopy!" Which sparks a comment about the canapés. I would love to dissect the jewel-like appetizers, but I follow the rule as if it will help me save my marriage. When the cake is served I've had too much champagne.

"I've never had better cake!" says the mother of the bride. "How did you find the baker?"

"The cake is perfect, is it not? The man knows about cake."

"But how did you know about him?" the woman asks again. I am glad she doesn't live nearby, that I will not have to talk with her often.

"I found him one ni—. Once," I say, "when I needed a cake for Petey's birthday. I don't bake," I confess, as if I still can't, and I put more cake in my mouth because I'm afraid of giving her the whole damn tale. Stories of affairs don't belong at weddings any more than talk of food belongs in my family.

"Yes, honey, how did you find the baker?" my husband asks. I hadn't realized he was at my side, but there he is, cupping my elbow, his eyes popping.

"Oh, you know, I heard a little something about him at the supermarket," I say. "Isn't it nice to have the sky as a canopy?"

"Yes," Gary says, letting go of my arm. I'm afraid he's going to lean me against a tree and get me to tell him all about the baker. "We are lucky."

Luck continues to bless me with a marriage of strict construction, and an equally structured affair. I become a grandmother. To a girl first, and then a boy. Petey and his family live an hour away and visit once a month on Sundays. We eat together, and I make things that kids will enjoy. When very small, the kids talk and whine about food, but by five, they are perfect guests. I show the baker pictures of Petey's family, and he loves to search the kids' faces for features that are mine. He doesn't seem to love me any less as my appreciation of food stretches over more and more of my life and body. Once, as a joke, I buy tulle and fashion us tutus.

"For old times' sake," I say.

"Oh, you shouldn't have," he says, but he puts it on, and we dance like teddy bears.

"Please," my husband says one evening, a piece of meat (heirloom variety cattle cut into a New York strip steak) on a fork, dipped in brown butter, poised in front of his mouth, "please tell me about this food."

I shake my head no and he screams. He throws the fork on his plate and I watch him, a monster of my creation. He pushes away from the table, pulls the cloth and everything on it to the floor.

"I want to know about the food! Why is the food so good? What have you done over the years? Please, tell me; that rule is stupid!"

He stamps his feet up and down. I shake my head no.

"A rule is a rule," I say.

"Well, I'm sick of it. I'm sorry I ever made it. I want to talk about food. What else do we have to say?"

"There is the weather," I suggest.

"Acquaintances can chat about the weather," he says. "If we don't start talking about everything, including the food, I will leave."

I cannot live with him any other way than I have.

"Then we must divorce," I say, and we do.

Irreconcilable differences is the reason. Even if he suspects that my secret is bigger than food, he knows better than to bring the subject into the courtroom. He can't tell strangers about the rule we used to build our relationship.

Gary moves near Petey. He lets the kids talk about food, the boy and girl tell me, as if I should make him enforce the rule.

Once my husband is gone, the baker expects to become mine, but I am not interested in more than what I have had. Granted, my husband's side of the bed calls me like an unread book, but I enjoy the lack.

The baker is dejected that I will not share my bed, or give up my house and move in with him. He threatens me, but I have my limits. Petey is, I think, offended by my behavior. I think he thinks I ought to move in with the baker, too. Legitimate things, get them out in the open.

But things are open enough for me. I love the rhythm of loving a man in the middle of the night at his job. If he came home with me, everything would become different. The kind of love I'd have for him here would be husband love, not lover love, uncomplicated by domestic issues. I could no longer fuck him.

In the daytime, after my nap, waking up with a cup of coffee, I like to think of my baker, of dancing in his arms in the summer with the door open to cool us off. Opera spills out of the speakers and la-la-la's trill from the baker's throat. We turn off the lights and stick candles in the rising dough. He dances me out in the street.

Sometimes, I like thinking of us almost as much as being us. I wonder if I would be so happy were I only to imagine this life, instead of living it. Instead of following the music in the middle of the night and learning how to bake.

The Butter, the Bottle, the Sugar Bowl
by Michele Battiste

Some things melt when not kept properly—
chocolate, lipstick, a halo.
He slouches in the kitchen, shirtsleeves rolled
to the elbow, a stick of butter warming in
his hand. (She smiled once, to find him
        like that, her dress wrinkled from the drive
        to get the good bread, her mouth slicked
        magenta, her giggle—a halo.) Already,
the wine is opened, his mouth a sponge, the bottle
spilling, the butter—a thorn.

She is in his city
somewhere. (She never waited for dessert, ruined
        her mouth with chocolate before the bread.
        If there was no chocolate, she'd dip her finger in
        the sugar bowl, her mouth—a halo, her giggle
        a scratch.) He unwraps the butter, grabs
the bread, wonders what the grain feels before the cutting,
before the butter thins, melts into and below.

A Writer Makes Cookies
by Patsy Anne Bickerstaff

Sunlight glitters through the window, on the rim of the four-quart glass mixing bowl. It is the largest of the set, the one I use to soak altar linens in oxygen bleach, when it is my turn.

Today, two quarter-pound sticks of butter form an X in the bowl. As they soften, one curves sensually upward along the sides; the ends of the other droop languidly, embracing. I am momentarily shocked, as if the butter, left to its own devices, might do something indecent. Briskly stroking, I stir it with the wooden spoon. Reaching to the stove, I twist two knobs. A red light appears, and the oven begins to warm, filling the kitchen with the scent of cinnamon left from another baking.

Brown sugar packs tightly down to the three-fourths level of the measuring cup. Turned over, it forms a neat mound on the base of shining butter, like castle towers built with sand buckets by children on the beach. I pour over it an equal measure of granulated sugar, a snowstorm that confronts me with a miniature mountain tableau. Stirring, blending, beating, I tease it to a creamy, fluffy mass.

A teaspoon of vanilla, its exotic fragrance rivaling the cinnamon aroma, spills over the pale-yellow, gleaming contents of the bowl, and disappears with a few whisks of the spoon.

Now, the eggs: grasping the perfect, white shells, admiring their heft and smoothness, and with only a moment's thought of the birds they will never become, I tap them against the bowl—one, two—emptying them into the mixture. The fat yolks stare at me in surprise, and a "ping" from the oven tells me it has reached its goal, 350 degrees.

With the eggs stirred into the creamed sugar and butter, the mixture is about to become dough. Twice, the measuring cup is filled, and soft, feathery flour poured into the sifter. A teaspoon each of salt and baking soda are added, and buried neatly beneath a final one-fourth cup of flour. I crank the handle of the sifter, stopping only briefly to turn the wooden spoon. The mass becomes firm, but still pliant; tempting, and a little dangerous, with its dramatic combination of traditional foodstuffs and chemically-produced catalyst—the most ancient and the most mysterious of seasonings. It will continue to combine even more ingredients, which at one time would never have met.

Chocolate, once the exclusive property of the rulers of undiscovered kingdoms, the secret of an unknown world, now easy to find in supermarkets, spills from its bright-yellow bag in delectable morsels, which are dispersed in the dough…all but a few, which I traditionally taste for quality, knowing full well the quality will always be the same, and always meet my approval.

Finally, I fill the measuring cup once more, with walnuts from the home of my ancestors. Their crisp, solid richness will be the perfect companion to the passionate, melting chocolate from the land of Moctezuma and Quetzalcóatl, the omnipresent sugar from the domain of Kamehameha, salt from a thousand secret places, vanilla from South American jungles, and wheat, butter and eggs that have always provided humanity with sustenance, everywhere. I place the dough by teaspoonfuls on my baking sheet, and into the hot, dark oven.

In ten minutes I shall take all credit for the irresistible result. Without one word about the kings and gods of Mexico, farmers laboriously tending their hens and cows and wheat fields, workers in salt mines, chemists making pure sodium bicarbonate, or explorers discovering the use of a long bean from a foreign bush; without a nod to the first Englishman brave enough to crack and taste a walnut, or the hotel chef whose exquisite skills designed the recipe, I shall present myself as genius, magician, all-powerful goddess, to someone who loves and trusts and believes me:

"Guess what Granny made for you."

Following the Recipe
by Sue Taylor

The Cake Bible says, "In a large mixing bowl combine all the dry ingredients and mix on low speed for 1 minute to blend." Kathy and I, we follow the directions, we put the 6 cups of sifted cake flour, 3 cups of sugar, 2 tablespoons plus two teaspoons of baking powder and 1½ teaspoons of salt in my mother's largest mixing bowl, the one that's been sitting, gradually filling with dust and animal hair, on the top shelf of the kitchen cabinet since my family moved to this house when I was nine. Then we stand there, looking doubtfully at the blades of the mixer as they stab down into all the fluffy whiteness.

Are you sure we're supposed to turn the mixer on with just the dry stuff? Kathy asks.

It's what the book says, I say, and I flip the switch right as she bends her head down to look more closely at the bowl. A small mushroom cloud of cake flour blooms up and hits her in the face.

Shit, I say. She looks at me, her face whitened like a geisha's.

You look like a geisha, I tell her.

Why'd you do that? she asks, putting her head down over the sink and wiping the floor off with her hands.

Accident, I reply, and duck into the refrigerator for the good bottle of champagne I've been chilling for us to drink while we bake this cake. I have a couple of bottles of cheap stuff for after we're drunk. This is a special occasion, worthy of celebration, our friend Zach getting married and us baking a wedding cake for 150 people, especially since neither of us has ever baked anything more complicated than Betty Crocker Fudge Brownie Mix. But this should be a simple matter of following instructions.

I grab a kitchen towel and flap it at the tiny particles of dry cake recipe floating in the air, then grab the champagne in a stranglehold and pop the cork, which flies off into a corner of the kitchen.

I think we have to remeasure, she says, tapping the bowl.

Oh, come on, it wasn't that much, I reply, but then I realize she's right, we can take no chances with something this complicated.

Yeah, we should do this totally by the book, I say, and pull the measuring cup out of the sink. I dry it with the dishtowel and open another box of cake flour. Glancing out the window, I realize it's dark enough to see the meteor shower that's on the sky's schedule this evening.

Hey, I ask, want to drink our first glass and watch the stars? She grabs two Burger King glasses out of the cupboard and stands there as I pour Veuve Cliquot into them, carries them to the door, and then turns back and says, Bring the bottle.

I bring the open bottle and another one, too.

The two of us sit on the ground outside, toasting Zach and his imminent marriage every way we can think of. We toast Jenny, whom neither of us really knows, we toast the new house just down the block from his parents' house, we invent and toast their future children, a pudgy, bratty little blond girl, the kind who waits until no one's looking and then squeezes packages in the supermarket until they pop, and a skinny red-haired boy, who will spend high school leaning out of speeding cars to whack mailboxes with a baseball bat and then grow up to be a Republican. We clink glasses and drink deeply each time, slopping champagne onto the ground. We drink to Zach's not drinking any more. I open the second bottle and send the cork popping off into the dark.

There's something I've always wanted to know, probably because it's none of my business.

Kath, do you ever think about how it would've been? She knows what I'm asking about.

I would never have made it through school, she tells me, I'd be stuck here, with a malnourished, neglected kid, in a singlewide trailer. I'd be the night clerk at the Circle K.

I can see it, a white aluminum-sided trailer swelling in the heat of summertime, dark oil patches staining the ground outside, broken plastic toys scattered on the floor inside, Zach's truck fishtailing up a dust storm as he leaves, split seconds before she could.

She probably made the right decision.

We sit for a while, listening to the bubbles in our glasses rise and burst.

He's off our hands now, I finally say, and with that, Kathy and I clink glasses one more time and look up at the sky.

It's quiet. The night is soft, there is a velvet deepness to it, and the stars shine like punctures letting light into an immense dark tent. I see a star curve downward across a corner of the sky, an instant of light and motion becoming one, and I point to it, but it's gone before she turns her head.

Back in the kitchen, we decide to mix the dry stuff by hand. We then add, in the sequence dictated by the book, nine large egg whites, two cups of milk, one tablespoon of vanilla, and one and one-half cups of softened butter.

Oh, crap, we forgot to preheat the oven, says Kathy.

That shouldn't be a big deal, I say, and look at the beginning of the recipe again.

"Arrange 2 oven racks as close to the center of the oven as possible, with at least two inches between them," says the book, "preheat the oven to 350." I eye the interior of the oven. I look at the oven racks. They seem far enough apart to me. I scrape some of the black stuff off the oven floor with my fingernails, then turn the dial to 350.

This'll work, I tell Kathy, let's get this cake in the oven so we can go back outside. She drains her glass, then tosses it into the sink with a sharp clatter that makes me wince, and switches on the Mixmaster. Attracted by the noise, my mother wanders into the kitchen. She stands there with her reading glasses sliding down her nose, looking at us.

Is this as far along as you two are? she asks, looking at the chicken-roosting-on-eggs clock over the sink.

We had some unexpected occurrences, I say.

Well, you better hurry up, she says, you don't have as much time as you seem to think. She pushes her glasses back up with one finger and pads out of the kitchen.

We're on our own schedule here, old woman, Kathy says as soon as my mother is safely out of earshot. I snort. We're slaves to the Cake Bible's schedule or we're going to be at the bakery section of the supermarket as soon as it opens tomorrow morning, pulling little plastic clowns off birthday cakes and assembling a Frankencake.

The book says to grease the spring-loaded pans and line the sides with parchment. Using both seems like overkill, but we're following the recipe now, no matter what. We carefully pour the exact amount specified by the book into each pan, and into the extra pans for emergency use. We have enough raw yellow butter wedding cake for two three-tiered cakes, just in case. We gently, painstakingly, slide the first of the pans into the oven, set the timer for the required 20 minutes, and take another bottle of champagne outside.

Will we hear the timer from out here? Kathy asks, holding out her glass. I fill it, champagne seething up over the top and dripping off her hand onto the ground, and look up at the sky. It is limitless, a deep black pulling me upward, the stars scattered like lost diamonds. An ant crawls up the top of my foot, and I brush it off.

Sure we will, I tell her, and fill my own glass to overbrimming.

A Brief History of Toast
by Angus Woodward

Toast comes in many varieties. You've got your fifteen-year toast, your ten-year toast, and your five-year toast. I don't recommend the five-year.

The Toast Hall of Fame in Bisbee, Arizona displays fourteen slices of presidential toast and pays tribute to a host of toast pioneers, including Hal Sponson, developer of toast on a stick; John Shoulderblade, credited with being the first to butter both sides of toast; Bette Smoonterly, patroness of many turn-of-the-century toast painters; and of course Jacques Serving, Canadian inventor of French toast (which the British call "eggy shingle").

Toast was actually created long before bread came on the scene. Individual pieces were cooked over open flames or in special dung-fired kilns for centuries before Isaac Loaf, the Earl of Bread, hit upon the idea of forming toast dough into logs, toasting it, then slicing the finished product. Society was amazed at the softness of "raw toast," as they called it, and bread, as it came to be known, soon appeared as a lining in hats, a stuffing for couch cushions, and a padding for the earliest dentist's chairs.

Toast theorists predict that the toast of the future will contain special whole-grain microchips that may be programmed to produce optimum texture, temperature, and brownage for each slice.

In Laos, toast is made from a crude metal derived from the mineral-rich soil unique to the region.

In 1744, during the Greco-Samoan war of 1612, Samoan warriors outfitted themselves with armor, hatchets, and shoes fashioned from crisp whole wheat toast. The outcome of the ensuing battle with Greek battalions has become the stuff of legend: using giant parabolic mirrors, the Greek army charred the Samoan toast and carried the day.

A primitive tribe in the Amazon basin uses toast as currency. Along the coast of that continent, many fishermen use toast as bait for yellowfin tuna. The Eskimo language contains 47 words for toast. In the U.S., many housewives keep a slice of toast handy in the kitchen for striking matches, scrubbing pots, and scaring away vicious hounds. Several pieces of toast were left behind on the moon by astronauts in the early 1970s.

The American Toast Council's advertisements have been a source of entertainment for years and have introduced catchphrases such as "love that scratchin' sound!" to daily language.

The world record for throwing toast is 713 feet, set by Georgia Plains of Plains, Georgia.

The Catholic Church recognizes the religious significance of toast.

For the artist, toast presents special opportunities. Subtle variations in temperature, voltage, and wind speed produce an endless variety of hues and textures. Through manipulation of such variables and the application of tinted butters, jams, and oils, artists have achieved breathtaking results. Witness such famous slices as "OK at the Shootout Corral" and "Can I Never Explode?"

It is impossible to imagine a context in which the adjective "nefarious" can be applied to toast. Can we say the same for crackers?

Skimming Off the Top
Tasting Yogurt in World Cultures
by Barbara Cunliffe Singleton

In Kashgar in the "Far West" of China I hear a cart-driver, stick in hand, shout, "Uh, uh! Want a ride?" The flowered canopy of his four-wheeled cart covers a platform spread with felt. Passengers are sitting, backs to center, their legs dangling over the sides. The heads of the younger women are bound by the shimmer of translucent scarves, the fashion of this Muslim city. My friend Aipasha shakes her head, swinging her gold earrings crazily beneath her glossy hair. We wave and the cart jingle-bells on.

We stroll past a boy selling honey ice cream from an enamel basin. He's been discovered by clamoring children and by bees that swarm and buzz. The boy shoos them away and they stay shooed—at least for a blink of a bee's eye—then hum back. Seeing Aipasha and me, the boy fills two glasses. We take them, happy as bees, swallow, and then, to be polite, swarm for seconds.

What I see next makes me realize we put the dessert cart before the main course, because there crouches a vendor, veiled in brown rayon, presiding over a tower of ceramic bowls of yogurt—each partly covered from the dust by a square of wood. When we buy two bowls from mid-tower, the woman gathers up her full skirt to where her flowered pantaloon meets her stocking. She reaches under the knee of her stocking and finds change for my 1-*yuan* note.

Aipasha and I scrape the skin from the top and savor the sheep-milk yogurt. Thick like soft cheese and tingling! (No "fruit at the bottom," but in stead a few flecks of brown glaze.) Feeling fit and well nourished to have eaten this zingy yogurt, I return the bowl with gratitude.

ತಿ

Thud!—Thud !—Thud!—Thump! pounds the room in a Buddhist temple in Lhasa, Tibet. Women seem to improvise on the beat, singing a melody. Curious, I peek into the dim room. Ten women hoist heavy poles—each based in a stone disk. They stick them into a wet floor of grit, smashed almost as smooth as concrete. As they thrump their disks, the women kick and side-step in a line.

A woman waves me in and, smiling, hands me a pole. Good! I whump my disk in rhythm, watching the feet of the woman to my left, and dance along, lacking only a long black dress and black braids to be one of them.

Half the group rests and sings, while the others dance. I can see why. The pole weighs a ton. The women smile when I meet their glances. I've muddled through work dances in my university folk dance group, but this dance is the real thing.

After my group dances and thuds the floor for three stints, I decide to stop before I'm arrested for working on a visitor's visa. I say "Thank you" in Tibetan and return the pole. Some smile, others look serious—taking a dim view of my stamina or, more likely, broken hearted that I won't finish the floor myself.

The woman who danced beside me follows me out of the room and we start down the stairs to the street level. I grip the steep wooden handrail, polished and worn, as I plunge down the deep risers to each narrow step. Yak butter candles balm the air with warm fragrance from the hall below.

On the street I smell the burning juniper whose sacred smoke lifts prayers to heaven. My "dancing partner" stops to speak with one of the girls who sells yak-milk yogurt in what look like pickle jars. The woman turns and speaks her first words of English to me. "My sister," she says, indicating a teenager whose black eyes melt in a little smile under delicate herringbone eyebrows. Dressed in a warm brown sweater, topped with a coarse black dress, she skims the top of the yogurt and hands it to me. I pay for it with Chinese money, and saying farewell to the group, I return to the Banak Shol ("furred skin") Hotel. Later, I relish my prize—prickly and smooth, rich with cream—a peaceful contemplative yogurt.

Inside the Kala Art Academy in Goa, a gray stairway leads up to the *trompe l'oeil* stairway of an imaginary rooftop. Yet visitors are not cheated. They can really go to the second floor of the Charles Correa-designed building and don't have to walk up a painting of stairs. Over the balustrade of an illusory balcony a muralled man leans his weight while perhaps thinking weighty thoughts. Out of his sight, portraits of men in wide-brimmed hats and overcoats exchange views, possibly about the current theatrical performance.

On the ocean side of the Academy, real second– and third-floor classrooms open onto terraces that project farther and farther, as if the building itself surged toward the sea in squares and rectangles.

Sitting at a table for tea on the ground floor, I see a breathtaking pattern and shade from the ceiling of recessed squares. I move from table to table to see the design from other vantage points. Striking patterns of dark and light form as I move.

I order tea and yogurt and fall into conversation with a white-haired Indian at a neighboring table. Dressed in white *khadi* (hand-spun cloth) with a multicolored *khadi* scarf, his face looks dark, bringing to focus one piercing eye. His other eye, impaired, follows the motions of the first like a slow brother. The man speaks about the hand-loomed clothing he wears. "People are not using a *charka* so much for spinning thread these days. During our struggle for independence, over sixty years ago, nearly every home in my town used a spinning wheel and loom, so we could weave *khadi* and boycott British fabrics."

The Indian, holding his tea glass, waits for a friend to pick up their free passes to use the railways for one year, a special benefit for freedom fighters. When he was a student in the South, the man says, "I cut wires, burned buses, cut railroad tracks. We students stole mailbags and burned them. We persuaded people not to pay taxes. On village walls and city buildings, we painted, 'Quit India!' as a warning to the British." His face shines with happiness, remembering.

His dark hand draped in white lifts his tea glass to gray lips. I try the soft chunks of *kurd* that sprawl, partially formed, on a stainless steel plate before me. The creamy dish tastes so good, it must be dense with carbonated fizz. How refreshing! From the yogurt, water separates onto the shiny metal.

I part from the gentleman, leave the restaurant and pause at the Academy auditorium. The front wall shows a river scene of what the theatergoer would've seen if no theater had been built. As I take a last look around, live crows peck on the dewy grass and sitar music from the practice rooms sounds through the arcades. I listen to the subtle glide of melody all the way to the front sidewalk, where an Indian woman wearing a white lab jacket approaches me.

Inserting a new questionnaire into her clipboard, she asks, "How would you rate the yogurt in the Kala Academy among yogurts you've tasted in other parts of the world?"

I hesitate, surprised, and allow my taste buds to compare the exact flavors. "My enjoyment depends upon the culture I'm in. As always, the most recent yogurt has the most kick." Smiling, she tilts her head from side to side and "ticks off" the answer.

Breakfast
by WILL WALKER

Reach down the Hadley bowl from the top shelf
in the pantry, the blue one with the ship
(three masts, square-rigged) sailing solidly
on a sea of alternating squiggles of blue and green,
pennants flapping off the masts, two seagulls
and an ornamental cloud the size of a little
free-floating sail decorating the fair skies.
Place the wide, shallow bowl on the plastic counter
and spin it so the ship sits upright
on its small stretch of sea. Then dish in
a little less than half a cup of Bran Buds and cover
with a hearty mound of Great Grains Crunchy Pecan cereal.
Open the new fridge with the seal so tight
it inhales sharply when you pull its hefty handle,
lift out West Soy Plus vanilla and pour on
sufficient soy milk to drown the ship and most of the rest,
leaving a tiny wetland bog of cereal and soy.
Then pad to the living room in your slippers and robe,
turn on Martha Stewart, and slurp to the sight
of today's guest chef demonstrating cooking in a wok.
First recipe, eggs fluffed up in the smoking peanut oil,
then piled high with Australian lobster tail
and exotic greens. You drain the swamp
with your favorite oversized silver-plated spoon,
then leave Martha and the wok brigade
as you shuffle back to the sink, now nearly ready
to sail into the squalls of another day.

Comfort Food
by Ann Hood

These are the things I remember:
    My five-year-old daughter Grace loved cucumbers sliced into perfect circles, canned corn, blueberries, any kind of beans, and overly ripe kiwi. A family vacation to southern Italy had left her with a taste for lemons and kumquats. She carried hard, dried salami in a small pink and white gingham purse and liked to go with me to Italian delis for fresh buffalo mozzarella. Her favorite dinner was pasta—*noonies*, we called it, a leftover mispronunciation from her older brother Sam when he was a baby—with butter and freshly grated parmesan cheese. Every day she took the same thing for her school lunch: prepackaged cheese and crackers, those cucumber rounds, half sour pickles. When her friend Adrian came over for lunch they always ate Campbell's Chicken & Stars soup, Ritz crackers, and either pomegranate or kiwi.

While I cooked dinner, Sam and Grace both helped me. They layered the potatoes for potatoes au gratin—*cheesy* potatoes in our house; they peeled the apples for apple crisp, the carrots for lentil soup; they shook and shook and shook chicken in a baggie of salted flour for chicken marsala. Grace used to like to press her thumbprint onto peanut butter cookies to flatten them before baking.

These are the things I remember: a fire in our kitchen fireplace, soup simmering on the stove, Sam and Grace bursting in with their cheeks red, their snowsuits wet, dripping snow across the wooden floor to snack on pickles straight from the jar before heading back outside. Or: our first backyard barbecue of the year on a surprisingly warm April day, Sam at eight finally old enough to baste the chicken on the grill, Grace carefully wiping a winter's worth of dust from the patio table and chairs, paper plates decorated with red cherries, the smell of molasses and brown sugar from the pot of baked beans, a bowl of canned corn dotted with butter, late afternoon sunshine, the purple heads of crocuses announcing themselves in our small garden.

What came the next day is the hardest part, the details of it impossible to forget. Grace spiked a high fever and, after thirty-six hours in the intensive care unit at our city's Children's Hospital, she died from a virulent form of strep. April remained relentlessly warm and sunny, but inside our house I shivered uncontrollably. Wrapped in flannel blankets and shawls from vistors, I could not find comfort. This was the unthinkable, the thing every parent fears. And it had come to our house and taken Gracie. When I looked out the window, I wanted her to still be there, making bouquets of chives from the garden laced with purple myrtle. Or when I walked in the kitchen, I expected to find her there, standing on her small wooden chair, plucking one cucumber round after another from her pink plate into her baby teeth filled mouth.

People brought food. Chicken enchiladas in a throwaway foil roasting pan and rich veal stew simmering in a white Le Creuset pot and cold cuts and artisan breads and potato salad and fruit salad and miniature tarts and homemade chocolate chip cookies and three different kinds of meat loaf and three different kinds of lasagna and chicken soup and curried squash soup and minestrone soup. It was as if all of this abundance of food could fill our emptiness.

We sat, the three of us left behind, and stared at the dinners that arrived on our doorstep each afternoon. We lifted our forks to our mouths. We chewed and swallowed, but nothing could fill us. For months people fed us and somehow, unimaginably, time passed. Summer came and friends scattered to beaches and foreign lands.

One day, gourmet ravioli filled with lobster and a container of vodka cream sauce appeared on our doorstep with a bottle of Pinot Grigio. Our garden was in full bloom by now. Hot pink roses. Ironic bleeding hearts. Columbine, and unpicked chives topped now with purple flowers. I carried the bag into my quiet kitchen and thought through the steps for cooking pasta. Somehow, the process that had once been automatic had turned complicated. Get a pan, I told myself. Fill it with water. I had not done even these simple things in almost three months. Yet soon the water was at an angry boil, the sauce simmered in a pan beside it. The simple act of making this food felt right.

The next day, I once again set a pot of water to boil. But instead of expensive pasta, I filled it with the medium shells that Grace had loved. When they were al dente, I tossed them with butter and parmesan cheese. That night, as the three of us sat in our still kitchen, the food did bring us comfort. It brought Grace close to us, even though she was so far away. Crying, I tasted the sharp, acrid tang of the cheese. It was, I think, the first thing I had tasted in a long time.

We think of comfort food as those things our mother fed us when we were children. The roasted chickens and mashed potatoes, chocolate cream pies and chewy brownies. But for me, now, comfort food is cucumbers sliced into circles. It's chicken and stars soup with a side of kiwi. It's canned corn heated to just warm. In losing Grace, there is little comfort. But I take it when I can, in these most simple ways. On the days when grief grabs hold of me and threatens to overtake me again, I put water on to boil. I grate parmesan cheese and for that night, at least, I find comfort in a bowl of noonies.

Not long ago, I was in the supermarket and a small basket of bright orange kumquats caught my eye. I remembered the trip to Italy when Grace developed a taste for these funny fruit. I could almost picture her in the front seat of my shopping cart, filled with delight at the sight of kumquats. I reached into the basket of fruit and lifted out one perfect kumquat, small and oblong and orange. When I bit into it, tears sprang into my eyes. The fruit's skin is sour, and it takes time before you find the sweetness hidden inside.

Two Poems
by Elisa Albo

Love, Wounds and Soup

I.

My mother slices the pale shells of onions
into a pot. Steam transports the oily scent
of thickening chickens, beans and bay leaf
through the air and out into the den where
I play jacks on the carpet, through the open
window and out to the walk where my father
in his long white lab coat approaches. I run
to the door, burrow my nose into the stiffly
starched folds, the clean, sterile hospital smell
of the Sunland Training Center in Gainesville.
Fresh dots of blood spot the sleeves he lets
slide off as he bends toward my mother, that
moment—when poised like a drop of water
that reflects the earth about to fall off its axis—
a whole world passes between them in a kiss.
He sits down to soup, black beans and rice,
olives, cheese, Genoa salami, salad greens.
As he eats, he feeds me, his hands big and
rough in spots from scrubbing for surgery,
exploring bodies, making delicate repairs.

II.

One day a recently opened and emptied can
of black bean soup beckons from the edge
of the high kitchen counter. Reaching up,
I slide my four-year-old finger past the jagged
teeth of the still attached lid, slurp the rich
black broth. On my second try, the lid bites in,
grabs my skin, spots of blood drip to the linoleum.
From the front seat of his old Chevrolet, my father
explains the entire procedure for mending my finger
en route to the hospital. In a sea of green sheets,
I still kick and scream, but once home eat my bowl
of black beans, tears adjusting the seasoning.

III.

The scar on my finger is a half-moon surprise,
on my belly and neck, thin curved lines. Over
the years, the results were often benign. On
the same finger, another oval scar, cut slicing
a wedge of Manchego, a gift from my mother,
like the solace of her soup, her savory black
beans. At home, she fed, he mended—he fed,
she mended. I grew tall, hungry, and whole.

Raising Kids

The day I announced I was running away,
my mother packed my lunch. Peanut butter
or egg salad? she asked, quickly untying

the bread bag, quashing the footsteps of Huck
Finn, Oliver, and Johnny Tremain. Brown
sack in hand, I trotted across the neighbor's

backyard, dropped down into the grassy lane
between the back fences and into the coolness
of their shadows. Blades of Bermuda grass

pricked my thighs. I opened a book, read a few
fairy tales, sipped a Coke with my crustless
sandwich. Picking a weed, I chewed its bitter

stem, watched for ants, lay back on the ground
and stared at the blue. What else was there to do?
I packed up and ambled home. My mother was

chopping yellow onions, sautéing them in olive oil.
I set the table the way she had taught me—forks
on the left, knives on the right, blades turned inward.

Cheap Food
by Susie Paul

for Helen Scott Paul

Apples, small and bruised, by the bag marked down. My mother
    Fried them to a pulp, like clotted meal.
Beans, white, not navy, but Great Northern, dried; she
    Soaked them overnight, cooked them 'til they
Creamed, gave up tiny worms, pink and curled like fetuses.
    My mother used three seasonings—salt,
    Pepper, and garlic salt. Thyme, or rosemary,
Dill, and marjoram, cumin were sadly foreign
    To her mountain repertoire, a menu
Endless in its permutations on cheap
Food. Still, she inherited this sense of the body's
    Need for balance, ballast.
Grits for supper to keep us full through sleep
    When not even
Hamburger was affordable that week.
I remember meals like formulae—cornbread
    With beans, or rice when we moved coastward; one
    Small chop, lots of tiny peas, Leseur; chicken wings—saved
    From many Sunday lunches, boiled until the flesh slid off the fragile
    Bones, purple with marrow—and dumplings. Salmon dumped from
Jazzy cans, the silver fish curving round, flounder, frozen, even
    When we moved coastward.
Ketchup on the table for the fish. My mother's
Lessons on economy were fed to us.
Money had

No power when she fried our steak, the least
    Expensive, toughest cut. Lean and mean, she pounded
    It with the saucer's edge until it
Opened into furrows, giving up its
Protein, feeding us, all three, all
Quivery,
Rangy children, blue-eyed, Anglo-Irish,
Scots, capable of meanness when required,
Tough,
Unyielding as our mother's eye for
    What sustains a body in a sometimes
Vicious world. A
Wasteland, the flatlands of the deepest South,
    For children with the mountains still rugged
    In their bones. My mother
Wrought us
Xeric, drought-proof,
Yet always thirsty, just hungry enough
    To range beyond our table.
    And the food she soaked and pounded,
    Simmered, tamed in
Zenic practice, answering us the mondo,
    Koan: When is sparseness never spare?
    When it feeds us.

Alphabet Soup Kitchen
by Ruth E. Dickey

Apples are not a good idea in soup kitchens. When I first became Miriam's Kitchen's director, one of my bright ideas was to serve fresh fruit, so I started ordering apples because they are cheap. I figured fresh fruit tastes a lot better than canned. But if you have dental problems, it's really hard to eat apples. Almost everyone who is homeless has dental problems, because the only free dental care available in DC is having your teeth pulled. So everyone hated my apples. Junior told me only an idiot would order apples. The only way that we could get people to eat them was to chop them up and add them to canned fruit salad, which Junior loved.

Bob was a member of the weekly poetry workshop I ran after breakfast at the kitchen. My favorite poem of Bob's was called "No More Streetlights in my House." After two years at the kitchen, I spent a year and a half in New Orleans. One day there I got a call at work from Bob. If you are homeless, finding a place to make even a local call is like trying to get a free ride on Giuliani's New York subway. I was sure the only reason Bob would be calling me long distance was to tell me that someone had died. On the contrary, Bob was delighted to explain he had just received a letter saying his poem, "Streetlights," was a winner in a contest. He could purchase the anthology in which it appeared for only $39.95. "And I'm going to use the $5,000 prize money for a deposit and first month's rent!" Years later, Bob still turned up sometimes at the kitchen. I never asked him about the money. I wanted to keep believing he'd won.

Cindy's face was instantly recognizable on the missing person flyer sent by the National Association for the Mentally Ill. I had seen her green eyes and tangled hair almost every day at breakfast for several months. In the picture, she looked cleaner and softer. I contacted her sister, Karen, whose number was on the flyer, and she sobbed when I called. Karen said she had been looking for Cindy for months. She said, "It's so hard. Everyone thinks I don't love my sister because she's on the street, but there's nothing I can do unless I can prove she's a danger to herself or others. And she's so paranoid she won't come home. Everyone thinks I'm a bad person. Do you?"

Down a set of concrete stairs, in the basement of a church, you can find Miriam's Kitchen. There are fifteen round tables with red folding chairs. The walls are covered with paintings by folk who eat breakfast at Miriam's, like Bob and Donald. On one side of the room are tables of cereal, juice, and milk/sugar/coffee. When you enter the room, you get a number that you will trade-in for your hot breakfast. Most people come every day, every day. Some come a few times a month. Others we see once or twice and never again.

Eggs were what we cooked every Monday and Wednesday. The lines were always longer on egg days. If 95 people had breakfast on Tuesday, 145 would eat breakfast on Wednesday. We usually scrambled the eggs. We had to remember to add a capful of vinegar to the raw eggs before cooking, otherwise they turned green in contact with the aluminum serving pans. Sometimes we added chopped tomatoes, ham, or green peppers, but always only to half. Some people get very upset if you put things in their eggs.

Frank was a junkie. I should have known because he always wore long sleeves, even in summer, and his hands were always dry and cracked, his shaking fingers yellowed from nicotine. But I hired him to help clean. He was always a very nice guy, friendly and willing to help unload the heavy cases of orange juice from the van or sweep the stairs. Frank frequently disappeared a day or two at a time, but eventually he just stopped coming to work. The rumor on the streets was that he had cancer and died. But you can't believe everything you hear. One day we were smoking outside and he said, "I'd like to find the guy who gave me my first hit, and I'd like to kill him. One hit was too many and ten million will never be enough."

George had too-bright eyes and liked to pump your hand up and down and up and down. He never liked to let go. He was about 6'4" and usually had grass or leaves in his hair. One day, I was walking towards Washington Circle, and George started walking with me. He was talking nonsense as usual, making me nervous. I told him I had to get to a meeting, and he grabbed me. I screamed; not a pedestrian stopped to help before I twisted away. When I called George's case manager to let him know, he told me George often grabs women when he's been drinking, and that I should set better boundaries. He said next time I should handle it better, next time I should call the police.

High-end food, liked smoked salmon, was not a big hit in our soup kitchen. We got donations of it a number of times—leftovers from fancy parties, unwanted Christmas presents. Giant fillets with capers and lemon wedges. We served it with eggs. The volunteers all drooled. Grandma, one of our sassier breakfast guests, said, "What the hell is that?"

Isabel was a volunteer who worked part time at Dean and Deluca and brought us candied lemon peel, praline sauce, and jars of roasted red peppers. Isabel looked at me one morning and said, "When it snows, I can't sleep, thinking of all of them outside." I tried to tell her that having a good breakfast in a friendly place mattered. That it made a difference. "It isn't enough," she said and excused herself to the bathroom to cry. The volunteer doing dishes had to leave early so I whispered, "It matters, it matters, it matters," to the rhythm of the dishwasher.

Junior was the street name of a guy who liked to stop by our office and ask, "When are you gonna get a real job? When are you gonna do some work around here?" Whether he saw me at work or on the street, this was always his greeting. He liked giving me a hard time. One summer night, I ran into Junior in front of a strip of restaurants and coffee shops on 17th Street. He was panhandling and I walked up to him and said, "When are you gonna get a real job? When are you gonna do some work around here?" He and I both burst out laughing. The other pedestrians shot me evil looks and one man muttered, "Bitch."

King, Carey King, was a bike courier and a talented poet. He often ate breakfast at the kitchen, and wowed our writing workshop with poems about old men trapped in their houses, the smell of spring, and unrequited love. Carey and another bike courier both OD'ed on heroin the same weekend in an unheated group house across from Malcolm X Park. Another outreach worker I knew, who spent his nights scouring alleys to give people blankets, said, "It must have been a good batch." We laughed like paramedics cracking jokes at the Rorschach patterns made by bloodstains. We laughed because the options dizzied us.

Lips are one of the first ways you can spot someone addicted to crack. While some regular crack users are stereotypically thin, many are not. Crack pipes can create a nasty burn on the lips, in the center. I kept noticing folks with scabs on their lips and thinking they'd been in fights or fallen down. When Queen had a nasty scab on her lip, I assumed her boyfriend had punched her. If you think about it, it's almost impossible to imagine people falling in such a way that they split the center of their lip.

Miriam's Kitchen was the name of the kitchen where I worked. People constantly asked if I was Miriam. Of course, it's a biblical story. Miriam was Moses' sister. She developed leprosy and was cast out. Later, she was miraculously healed and spent the rest of her days working with those who had been cast out. The kitchen was named for her as a safe space for those who have been cast out. These days, "those who have been cast out" are people sleeping on the streets. The kitchen was named twelve years before I arrived, but I got really good at telling the story.

Nate dressed in drag with a bouffant wig and huge, fake, clip-on pearls. People on the street called him Grandma. Grandma worked with a case manager to get disability and finally to get housing. It took about a year and a half. After about six months in housing, Grandma turned up at breakfast again. It seemed that Grandma couldn't agree with the no-alcohol rules in transitional housing. After a few months out and a trip to rehab, Grandma re-entered housing. I hoped it would last at least a few months.

Oscar never sat. He ate his breakfast standing with his back to the wall. Oscar also never spoke. From his age, and his insistence on never having his back turned, I guessed he was a Vietnam vet, as were about a third of our breakfast guests. I even guessed his name was Oscar. I said good morning to Oscar every day, and after a year and a half, one rainy Thursday, he said good morning back. I still don't know Oscar's story or his real name, but that good morning was a major victory.

Porter is the volunteer who led the pancake production on Tuesdays. Porter looks remarkably like Newt Gingrich, and the guys at the kitchen like to call him Mr. Senator. He's been coming to the kitchen ever since his daughter came with her church youth group 15 years earlier. Sometimes, to be different, Porter and his crew would make special pancakes—apple, chocolate chip, blueberry. But you always had to divide the batter and make half the pancakes plain. Some people get very upset if you put things in their pancakes.

Queen was her street name. Almost everyone on the streets has a real name and a street name, kind of a CB handle. I always thought that when you don't have much left, you don't want to give out your name. It's the last possession you have, in a way. So almost everyone had a street name. Queen got hers because she acted as if she ruled the streets, the parks, the kitchen, the volunteers, and anyone else who crossed her path. When she was high or in a pleasant mood, she was expansive and regal in spandex. When she was drunk, she was ferocious and nasty. When she was drunk, she liked to spit at me.

Rumors are thick in soup kitchens. Queen's boyfriend got locked up and the story on the street was that he stabbed a guy in the stomach. Junior told me another guy was locked up in John Howard for threatening the president. Frank told me Susan's family had millions of dollars. Donald told me a museum was going to buy his paintings and he'd be rich. Grandma told me George had chopped his first wife to bits. Bob told me Grandma turned tricks to buy vodka. Everybody had a story about everyone else, but my favorite stories were the ones about me. Grandma asked if it was true that our Social Worker and I were getting married because I was having his baby. And Frank asked if it was true that my parents are black and had adopted me, and that's why I wanted to work at a soup kitchen.

Susan was a skittish woman. She had eyes so blue, I kept thinking they should leak. She rarely spoke with anyone on staff, but she stayed at night with Frank the junkie. Frank told us she believed her family was pursuing her, with the help of the FBI and CIA. Susan and Cindy never spoke, but they had a lot in common. After Frank disappeared, Susan did too for a year or two. When someone disappears at a soup kitchen, it is either very good news (they got into treatment, got an apartment, reunited with family) or very bad news (they are locked up, in a hospital, or dead). The morgue routinely brought down snapshots for us to try to identify. When Susan resurfaced, she had a huge scar that almost completely circled her neck and extended up behind one of her ears, with a jagged line of black stitches. The morning she returned, she said hello to me by name for the first time.

Tito was the breakfast guest who stalked me in the morning. I had to be at the kitchen before the Metro opened at 5:30 a.m. I didn't have a car, so I walked to work every morning through dark streets. Tito liked to hang out along the routes I walked, and to follow me. He never actually hurt me; he just scared me. He also liked to bring me presents: little-girl plastic barrettes in red and yellow, tinfoil sculptures, a pink comb.

Urban Plunge is a program in which college kids spend 48 or so hours on the street, learning a bit about what it's like to be homeless, kind of like a vacation in being homeless. They were usually from somewhere in the midwest. Plungers, as they are known on the street, would turn up at breakfast because other people in the parks would tell them to come. They were always in groups, and no matter how shabbily they were dressed, you could pick them out by their shoes. We knew there was a good street network to tell new arrivals about the kitchen, because of the regularity with which plungers turned up. I always worried that some kid who was a runaway would get overlooked because we assumed he or she was on a plunge.

Vans are ideal for sleeping if there's no room at the city shelters. One winter, a family with three kids and a dog began sleeping in their van in the blocks close to the kitchen. Frank alerted us to their presence, and invited them to come down to breakfast. The wait for space at the emergency family shelter was 94 days when we called on their behalf. A neighbor became concerned and called the cops. The dog was promptly removed to an animal shelter. The family was told to find somewhere else (like Virginia or Maryland) to park their van, which I suppose they did since they disappeared.

Women and men with exaggerated eyes were the primary subjects of Donald's portraits, which were often done in craypas or crayon. When he was still sleeping outside, Donald hid his paintings in the bushes, in trashbags to protect them from the elements. The Park Service, not known for their art appreciation, were always cleaning out the bushes and discarding Donald's work. He often appeared at breakfast ranting about his stolen masterpieces. Donald also liked wine, preferring vintages under $3. One night after too much wine, Donald was hit by a taxi in Washington Circle. The story on the street is that Donald was dancing in traffic. After a long rehabilitation, Donald finally moved into housing. He died of an aneurysm a year and a half later; I took three buses to get out to Maryland to his funeral. His family proudly displayed Donald's paintings next to his casket, colorful portraits of Bette Davis and OJ Simpson sealed in saran wrap. The program described him as an artist and a poet. Three of the women there were crying.

X-rays are of great concern when you work with large numbers of paranoid or psychotic people. I was often told they are used by the government/FBI/CIA/police/aliens to watch us and gather information. Some people said the x-rays sent them messages, telling them what to do. Cindy told me x-rays are sent by the radar dishes on top of tall buildings, by individual radios which have been rewired by spies, by cell phones, by fillings in your teeth. George said you can never be too careful of x-rays.

Yellow was a ubiquitous color at the kitchen. The plastic food trays were yellow. The cereal bowls were yellow. The eggs, the grits, and Porter's pancakes all were shades of yellow. The canned fruit salad Junior loved, sliced oranges, and canned peaches all approximate shades of yellow once you've started to see things through the yellow lens. Hard core alcoholics, like Grandma, have a yellow tint to their eyes; smoking, coffee and crack turn your teeth yellow. Once you start looking for yellow, it's everywhere.

Ziploc bags are hot commodities at soup kitchens. They are useful for holding most anything: sugar stolen for later, a pastry or scrambled eggs for a snack, half-smoked cigarettes gathered from ashtrays in front of office buildings, cereal. They will keep these items dry in your pockets if you get wet, and keep the eggs from oozing down your legs. Ziploc bags are good for the things you will carry, and if you are eating breakfast at a soup kitchen, you will need to carry everything that is yours.

*Most names have been changed.

Thirteen Ways of Looking at a Nantucket Bay Scallop
by Annie Kay

1. A hundred blue eyes winking back.
2. Loch Ness eel, beady eye to mine. We reach together. I am gone.
3. If a scallop could run…snowy muscle battles blade.
4. He wooed me with the smell of you and garlic.
5. The only thing that can get me into Polpis Harbor in October.
6. Shells golden glow on holiday bough.
7. Wine, spinach, cream and nutmeg can't ascend without you.
8. Slicing guts goes slow in the numb, fridged twilight.
9. My landlocked Dad's favorite food on earth.
10. Pity them what can't tell you from rubber sea fatties.
11. Faster ferries, choking eel grass. We save time but no one will save you.
12. Best barefoot driveways.
13. Madaket closed. Sweet seed sleeps in peace.

Shad Chant
by Lawrence F. O'Brien

I will rise and go now and eat broiled shad and roe
because it is the brightest, bluest day in May
and because my New England ancestors ate shad
in May, when the slick, swollen fish swam in silver
multitudes up the Connecticut, and people served
shad breakfasts on clean town greens in the innocent
sun and white shirts of the nineteenth century
and because roe is the birth of new life, rich and heavy
and brown, broiled with the fat of bacon, pungent
with fertility and the strong, sharp salt of the sea
mixed with sweet, fresh inland earth and the cold,
plunging waters of the Connecticut, and I will gorge
on shad and roe and delight in the oil and grease
and hot, white flesh and bursting spawn on my palate
savoring, with relish, the deepest seeds of spring.

❦ *Dream of a Rarebit Fiend*
A Metamorphosis

by DONALD NEWLOVE

I lie on the big leather boat of my living room couch and mull over the recipe for the lobster risotto I plan to make for Madeleine Moontree when we dine alone at my apartment this evening.

Although I have already laid place settings for two, I am restless and should not have stretched out on the couch. I face a long afternoon in the kitchen before she arrives. And I admit it, perhaps I overdid lunch.

Some fiendish memory carried me off and stirred me to whip up a pot of my favorite Welsh rarebit or bastard fondue. This cold-weather recipe comes from the stony old streets of Zurich. It's a dish I adore after a walk on the old-town side of the Limmat River and after visiting the statue of Joyce in Fluntern Cemetery. Anyway, I wheedled the recipe from a chef in a little restaurant on a cobbled and hilly Zurich side street.

I won't spell out the classic recipe known by all but I'll say it takes butter, flour, Dijon mustard and Worcestershire and heavy cream and ale and a good whisk. In my version I pour a cup of heavy cream into a chafing dish and add a pound of grated four-year-old cheddar and a pound of grated nutty-sweet Swiss Emmenthaler and as the mix melts in the heated chafing dish in goes a bottle of woody India pale ale. I whisk without stop and bring all to a smelly melt on low heat just short of browning the muck. At the last moment I add a pound of grated *Parmigiano Reggiano*, because you can never have too much *Parmigiano Reggiano* on anything but perhaps Cheerios, and the dish becomes not strictly Swiss or Welsh but more of an international metamorphosis and rich and strange and ready for strips of rye toast. I'm afraid I licked the pot clean.

Next I know I've floated off the couch and gone to the kitchen to begin the risotto. I stand in the doorway. Someone has left the far kitchen door open. Who? Or did the door just blow open? A big breeze sweeps in. I keep hearing from my long butcher block this medley where the pots and pans hang and the breeze turns them into Swedish chimes. The shock of pots and pans singing almost keeps me from stepping into the kitchen. I wonder, Are my two three-pounders still alive in the tub I've put them into with the water running? Am I really hearing small voices cry, Mama! Mama! I really must get into the kitchen to check on my pricey big green crawlers. And do I have a pot big enough to put them both into at once? Where I can boil them as they comfort each other? And should I start the Arborio rice before I boil the lobsters or while the lobsters boil? The Swedish orchestra of the pots and pans grows. I wish I could get into the kitchen. But the noise is so strong. Am I even up to this dinner? Into the kitchen, Donald, step out. Put your foot in. You can do it. But something odd has joined the madness of the pots and pans. It's coming from the sink. Do lobsters speak to each other? I've actually never heard that scream they make when you put them into the pan. I mean, I always put them in head first. Some people, I guess, who put them in tail first hear the scream. This is the only off-putting thing about lobster risotto. Well, you want them alive when you buy them, so it's up to you to ...Well, you know. Who wants a limp, dead lobster in the fridge? Or two of them? And three-pounders! Be like a morgue.

I hear a melting voice out of nowhere say, Lie down, Donald.

I ask aloud, Did I hear someone?

Yes, I'm here to help.

Who are you?

My name is Winsor McCay. I am God of All Fondues, Rarebits and Bastard Cheese Melts! You have invoked me.

Where are you, sir?

Somewhere between the Emmenthaler and the *Parmigiano Reggiano*. I come to warn you that you have not had the full rest you need after a pot of rarebit and loaf of rye toast. You should lie down again.

But I must get into the kitchen. She'll be here and I'll not be ready.

Donald, to work now is not a wise choice. Go lie down again.

I gaze with longing at the forbidden kitchen. I can't hear the water running. Are my lobsters alive and in good health? But I turn and am back on the great leather boat of my couch. I've just stretched out and sunk through the leather when the couch lifts from the floor and passes through my casement window and I'm floating by the clock tower of the Jefferson Court House Library. Now I'm sure that my three-pounders will not be enough meat for Madeleine and me. Or for Donald's Risotto Paradiso. I need one last lobster. My little *tête-à-tête* with Miss Moontree must flower into a night we'll both remember and hunger to repeat.

My couch floats down Sixth Avenue toward the big fish markets at the tip of the island. Oh, they've moved! Must I go to Hunts Point in the South Bronx? What a long trip, even by couch.

But now I'm shaken by something I see. It's a feeler antenna smelling my couch and as I look over the edge I see in the East River a lobster as big as a ferry boat. And now it crawls onto the wharfs. I stare down the big feeler as a huge compound eye on a stalk stares at me through hundreds of joined lenses. Four smaller antennae keep ever-moving and then a gigantic crusher claw reaches up and grabs my couch and we begin a crawl up Sixth Avenue on the lobster's six walking legs as I look down at a vast carapace a half-block long and twitchy tail that goes on for fifteen minutes by foot-measure.

I can tell now by her extreme sensitivity that she's a female and in fact we are now standing before the Jefferson Library clock tower as her feelers sweep about my open casement window and smell my three-pounders in the sink tub. Damn! She wants her children back. And now her feelers have gone through my window and her head, such as it is, fills my living room as she screams to her kids under their running water. Bricks loosen as her cutter claw forces its way in and the feelers lead it to my sink.

No, no! I cry. These are for Madeleine!

And I leap off my couch under the sky and slither past claw-joints through my window and run toward the kitchen to save our supper. But as I race slower and slower through a tar pit and reach the kitchen doorway the head-ringing bang of pots and frying pans set ajar by the big claw swinging about the butcher block sends out waves that freeze my arms and legs. Nor do the waving cutter claw and feeler that jam the doorway leave me room to enter. At last I scream free and jump onto the joints of the claw and squeeze into the kitchen to fight for my Madeleine while from the sink I hear baby lobster screams for mama, who is clearly named Gertie, for my three-pounders cry out, "Gertie! Gertie!" And then my dinosaur-huge crustacean has them and holds them wriggling above my head as her claw and feeler withdraw from the kitchen and I see her claw's slow motherly slide slime the dining room carpet and knock my dinner chairs aside and send my place settings sailing as books tumble from their cases and the claw with its babes backs out my casement window.

Now all this may be hard to believe but to my delight my dear Madeleine, when she arrives, with a single glance takes in my slimed rug and drunken disarray of chairs and gives me the hug that my soul hoped would follow my lobster risotto.

And that, ladies and gentlemen, is how I won the woman of my dreams and a pot of rarebit turned into a giant lobster.

COFFEE BREAK

Coffee
by **JEHANNE DUBROW**

> *No coffee's better than the Polish brew.*
> —Adam Mickiewicz

We must believe the poet when he proclaims
that Polish coffee was the best and trust
his words about the shining, roasted beans.

Maybe the oily shells could make a drink
that wrapped the tongue in fur. It might be true
that silver spoons stirred sugar constantly,

that life was orderly as china cups
laid out in even rows, and elegant
as damask tablecloths that came from France.

But we have only gulped glasses of tea,
holding their metal handles with the tips
of nervous fingers, the water biting us,

its tang of rosehips, mint, or black currant,
enough to pucker any mouth and leave
the palate dreaming of Arabica.

We've swallowed quickly because time runs fast—
not like those ladies dressed in velvet gowns
who spent their days pouring from pewter pots,

not like the Polish poet, who must have lied,
writing his country as it should have been:
long, peaceful afternoons washed down with cream.

Drinking Lattes in Krakow
by Ellen Herbert

Advice to Starbucks: don't go into Poland. The best lattes I ever tasted can be found in the beautiful medieval city of Krakow. Their lattes begin with a bottom layer of frothy cream, a stratum of dark French roast espresso, topped with another layer of froth, served in a tall thick glass, so you can appreciate these layers. The glass is placed in a pewter server with a handle, so the drinker does not burn her fingers as she raises it to her grateful mouth. One barrista, my name for them not theirs, even made a heart design on the top of my cream in nutmeg and cinnamon. I got this same gorgeous latte all over town, in the fancy town square, Rynek Glowny, as well as in artsy Ulica Bracco near Jagiellonian University and in Kazimierz, the old Jewish quarter.

Being Starbucks trained, I had to learn new coffee etiquette in Krakow. The first couple of times I went into a café, I walked to the counter, ordered, then stood there and looked at the man or woman behind the counter.

I learned quickly that their English was quite good. They would smile and say forcefully, "Sit down." Coffee drink making is time consuming, and none of the makers wanted to be watched. They took their time, but so could I.

As far as I could tell, you can sit in a café and nurse a coffee all day. These cafés I might add offer seating on velvet or leather sofas. It was raining the day my husband and I stepped into the café in Kazimierz, where we found a wheat-colored velvet sofa. The waitress put my coffee down on the marble-topped table decorated with a bouquet of fresh flowers. The French window beside us was open to the rain. We sat for hours, sipping slowly and watching people pass on the cobbled-stone street.

This way I learned to adjust to the pace and rhythm of this city of castles and mounds on the serpentine Vistula. Krakow has experienced all the terror and domination the twentieth century had to offer, first the Nazis, then the Soviets—or Bolsheviks, as Cracovians call them. And now their city, a favorite spot for the rest of Europe and the UK, has been invaded by tourists. So the advice the café girl gave me early in our stay was good, "Sit down." Leave American hurly burly behind and sip the unique richness around you, but do so slowly. Here, you have all the time in the world.

How Birds Taught People to Make Coffee
—a Retold Cuban Folktale

by **Margarita Engle**

An old couple who lived in the forest noticed their goat eating red berries from a small tree. "Be-e-be, be-e-be," bleated the goat, and since 'bebe' means drink in Spanish, the old woman thought the goat was telling her to drink the red berries. She picked some berries, boiled them, and served the brew to her husband. "This tastes terrible," the old man said with a grimace. "That goat doesn't know anything about cooking." Just then, a guinea hen came along and clucked, *"Tostao, tostao,"* which means 'toasted.' The old woman tried toasting the berries, but they were still bitter. A cuckoo flew by calling, "moliiito," and since this sounded like *molido*, meaning 'milled,' the woman decided to try crushing some of the toasted berries in a small grinder. Still no improvement. Along came a crow, clacking, *"Colao, colao,"* which sounded like colado, meaning strained. So the old woman quickly strained the brew of ground, toasted berries through a piece of cheesecloth. "This still tastes awful," her husband complained. "Those birds don't know anything about cooking."

The woman was just about to give up when two doves landed on the kitchen windowsill, cooing, *"Azucar, azucar."* Smiling, the old woman thought, Yes, of course, azucar, sugar, that's what this bitter stuff needs! She added several heaping spoonfuls of sugar to a cup of the strong, dark brew.

"This is delicious!" her husband exclaimed. "Doves," he said, "are the best cooks in the forest. You should listen to them more often."

🍂 Interview with Joanne Harris

Joanne Harris is best known for her novel Chocolat, *upon which the popular 2002 film was based.* Chocolat *is the rich tale of a strange, magical woman who comes to a sleepy French village and transforms its people with her charm and her irresistible chocolate shop. In the book, chocolate becomes an alluring, curative, welcoming, and compassionate character. In subsequent novels,* Five Quarters of the Orange, Blackberry Wine, *and short stories collected in* Jigs & Reels, *Harris folds the power of food and drink into the deepest of human experiences and passions. Joanne Harris has also written two cookbooks:* A French Kitchen *and* The French Market, *and she's the author of other not necessarily food-centric novels:* Coastliners; Holy Fools; Sleep, Pale Sister; *and her most recent,* Gentlemen and Players. *We were particular interested in her masterful blending of food and fiction.*

How does food and drink come to figure so much in a lot of your work?

I think it's because I write about people and people tend to be universal. There are a number of things that bind people together and one of those things is what they eat and how they eat, how it affects their culture and the way they socialize and how it indicates what kind of a personality they have. I think that you can tell quite a lot about somebody by the way they relate to food.

You portray food, herbs, and drink as powerful talismans. Like the oranges that induce headaches in *Five Quarters of the Orange*, and the herbs for protection in *Blackberry Wine*.

This is something that has existed for centuries; the idea of the talismanic properties of foods and the things that grow. It's part of our folklore and our folklore, I think, is the central core of modern storytelling. So I think I'm tapping into something very old and also very universal. Everywhere in the world there are the same types of stories surrounding food and its magical properties.

If you look at great literature and at religious literature and folkloric literature, it all has that kind of central core running through it. You can start off with the Garden of Eden, if you like, and you can go through Dickens, Shakespeare, and Chaucer, and they all have food as important central areas.

Some of your characters seem psychically attuned to the properties of food and drink. Are these characters more open to these properties than others?

It *is* a question of openness. It's a question of embracing life, and a lot of the time I've used food as a metaphor for passion, for love and just for the love of life. The characters that don't like food, in my books, tend to be damaged in some way. They tend to reject warmth and they tend not to be able to connect with other people, because food is one of those things that enable people to come together, even people of different cultures, because it's such a simple thing to share, and everybody needs it. Everybody relates to it in more or less the same kind of different ways.

Your stories also have powerful artifacts pertaining to food. Like the coveted recipe journal in *Five Quarters of the Orange*, and Joe's spice cabinet in *Blackberry Wine*.

It's about the past. It's about keeping heritage and the past alive. In the case of the cookbook, it's about passing it on from previous generations. And in the case of the seed cabinet, it's more important than that, it's almost a kind of Noah's Ark. It's to stop important knowledge from being lost, and we all do this in our different ways. We do it in small ways and big ways, but it's something that we all hanker after, the wisdom of the past and ways of being able to pass on what we have done, what we've felt.

And recipes are one of those things that do get passed on because they are at the same time trivial and also very everyday and familiar. You always remember the smell of your grandmother's kitchen or of certain times of year when certain things were being cooked and it becomes part of your past. We forget these kinds of thing and it's a good thing to remember them.

And it brings the past alive into the present—Jay drinking the blackberry wine, Framboise cooking her mother's recipes. It creates a whole new world in the present.

That's right. So, basically, the people who passed on those things are never really dead because they're being remembered and certain things, certain rituals to do with food, are being acted out in their memory. It is almost a rite in one respect and it's also a gesture of love and of memory.

It's like something alive that you can carry around and then breathe life into it by putting it together again.

Yes. We tend to use food to designate who we are and where we came from. I think in America this is particularly true, because there are so many different cultures and one of the ways of keeping your culture separate and celebrating its diversity is through celebrating its foods and its customs. So, even if you're a very long way from where your family originated, there are certain customs that you can keep going.

You're part French and part English, yet you seem to have mostly French food references in your work. Is that the stronger part of your palate, so to speak?

Well, when I talk about France, I tend to talk about French food because French food has a very distinctive cultural identity which is linked to many of the things that I'm trying to put across. When I write about England, I don't tend to write about food in the same way at all because first up, my background doesn't contain as many of those references, and also English food has much less of a cultural identity. It has become much more fusion based and it's much more a kind of product of its cultural diversity than its own native culture.

Although, there is a native English food culture, no?

Yes, but it's disappearing because most of the traditional British food is not the sort of thing that people want to eat nowadays.

The restaurant that Framboise opens in *Five Quarters of the Orange* and Vianne's chocolate shop in *Chocolat*, both in small French towns, are such

appealing places. Do you fantasize about having a shop or restaurant like one of those?

No, not at all. I don't want to do it. But I think in France there is a much greater appreciation of good food. You know, people tend to take good food for granted because its something that has surrounded them. They have a great tradition of taking their time over meals and there's a great emphasis on quality. You don't get fast food franchises in France the same way that you do elsewhere because people just don't go there.

And so the atmosphere and the environment are terribly important and the people who run these places are very important, too, because French people are on first name terms with the owners of their local restaurant and their local café and their local shops. There is much more of a little village tradition even in the big cities. It is one of the things that has shaped the society of France.

And you explore that tradition so well in your stories. Jay in *Blackberry Wine* goes to the same French village where *Chocolat* took place. The reader gets to revisit the *Chocolat* characters at a later date. And we get a taste of what you just described—the village characters all know each other and know each other's histories.

France has a strong rural tradition. Even though it's got big cities, there are still an awful lot of these little villages with that very specific village mentality. It's something that I've explored over and over again, because it's so interesting to observe people who know each other so well and have a chemistry and evolve like that.

Is it their connection to what they grow and what they make that keeps them closer to a rural lifestyle? Rather than, say, buying food products from other places, like supermarkets?

Yes, that's right. There are areas in France where you will go a long, long way before you find a supermarket because people don't shop there. People have their own markets and they have them every day and they would not dream of going to a supermarket. Even where farming is the way of life, you still get an awful lot of people who reject the kind of large scale farming that brings them the most money. They are still working from little backyard kinds of enterprises, little strips of land and they're specializing in things that are traditional. These traditions are passed over from father to son over years and years. I was down there researching one of my cookbooks and it was very clear. You had these 80-year-old men who had inherited the vineyard or the olive grove or whatever from their father, and they were basically waiting for their 65-year-old son to be old enough to understand exactly what they're going to do before handing over the reins. It was wonderful.

It really seems important to you to communicate that kind of culture within the stories you tell.

I try to celebrate diversity where I find it and to emphasize the importance of the past and the importance of people doing things the right way, rather than the convenient, established way. And hanging on to identity, because it's very easy in the modern Europe to lose identity, there's so much centralization now. And being original and regional and a specialist just doesn't pay anymore. But you do get these stubborn characters who do it whether it pays or not, which is rather wonderful.

What about some of the recipes and dishes in *Five Quarters of the Orange* that seem to be from 1940s France? Were those specifically researched recipes from that time, or are they the same recipes you'd find now?

They're my family's recipes and some of them are much older than that. Some of the recipes in my cookbooks are from the 16th century, but they exist pretty much the same as they always have. This is the culture of French food. Most of it is peasant cooking and is based on regional seasonal ingredients. And they are things that pretty much everybody knows about in France. Everybody, every family has its own way of doing these things because you know, somebody has a special method and they pass it on, but basically, the dishes are the same.

So they are recipes from your own ancestors?

They're my grandmother's recipes and her mother's recipes and there's nothing new there.

Are there any writers whose writing about food has impressed you or impresses you now?

Well, to be honest, everybody writes about food. I mean, there had been a time of a few decades when people didn't write about it, because there was a sort of minimalist approach to style and there was this idea that writing about food was old-fashioned. But food writing is a kind of sensuality. It runs through our tradition of literature for hundreds of years. I suppose I've been influenced by that. I don't know any modern writers who do it quite in the way that I do, or that I was used to reading.

Your stories are so well crafted as stories that the food doesn't feel stuck on.

I don't tend to think of food as something I have to add on. If it's not an integral part of the story, then it won't be there, that's all. It the same with sex scenes, you know, they say you can't get away with publishing a book now that doesn't have a sex scene before page 40. Well, I haven't written a sex scene in my life because I've never felt it was entirely necessary within the story.

But I think that if you are writing about people, and that's really what I do write about, then a number of universals will come out of that and one of them is eating because, you know, everybody eats.

Conversation with Neruda
by Persis M. Karim

For Pablo, who keeps me ever amused

"Listen, Guapa, why are you eating alone in this cantina?"

"I'm eating *Sopa Azteca*," I tell the round-faced man who appears suddenly at my booth. "For my cold," I say, blowing my nose over the large, steaming bowl.

"*Sopa Azteca?* That reminds me of a story I want to tell you."

He tells me to call him Pablo and begins telling his story:

"That chicken soup, that's not just for sick people; it is the food of the gods! Once when I was writing a poem, an Aztec warrior stood at my desk and invited me for lunch. 'But I'm very busy,' I told this warrior. 'I'm writing a sonnet for my wife.' The warrior, whose name was Xtapolteca, banged his long spear so hard it made the leather flap of his *tabo rabo*—what you call a loin cloth—lift up in the air.

"I thought it sounded like a made-up name, but who was I to doubt this serious-looking X-warrior? 'Poems aren't made of paper and pen,' he told me." Pablo lets out a deep belly laugh and goes on with his story:

"'There are *too* many love sonnets, Neruda,' said the warrior. 'What we need is a different kind of poem, a poem about cilantro, socks, or *Sopa Azteca*.'"

The soup begins to make my nose run.

"Excuse me, Señor Neruda," I interrupt. "May I blow my nose?"

"Go ahead *Dulce*, but here comes the most important part."

At this signal, Pablo removes his cap and places it gently on the table.

"My warrior friend begins lecturing me. Me, the great poet, Neruda." Pablo raises his hands and eyebrows in unison. "'You people of the twentieth century, you are, what we say in my village, stiffer than the ruins of Palenque. You don't know how to dance, you don't know how to kiss in the streets. You're too worried. About producing, about money, about writing poems, about writing *great* poems. Forget your damn sonnet, Neruda!'"

Pablo shakes his head from left to right. His sad, basset-hound eyes grow larger.

"Can you believe it, *Carino*? Is he trying to say, that I, Pablo Neruda, am not spontaneous? He must have mixed me up with one of those gringo poets… Wordsworth, Eliot, or what's his name, Robert Frosty? 'Pablo, my dear, eat your soup and then you will understand,' Mr. X said and then disappeared.'"

"Well, so what happened?" I ask at this abrupt ending to the story.

"*Nada, Dulce.* Nothing." His face erupts into a smile. "I decided to write a few odes instead: Ode to the book, the socks, the tomato.

"It's up to you to write the ode to *Sopa Azteca*."

Three Meals
by Peter Selgin

These are the three best meals I have eaten in my life:

1. Paros, Greece. The little fishing village of Naoussa with its horseshoe harbor and colored boats. From the local store my fiancée Tatiana and I bought bread, olives, feta, sausage, grapes, a bottle of Demestica. With glasses and a sheet from our hotel room we walked to the bay and set a table made of fish crates. We ate as the sun set and stray dogs gathered around. We tossed them pits from the olives and skin from the sausage and never got married.

2. At one of my many cousins' villas in northern Italy, Maurizio, the caretaker, invited me to lunch with him outdoors. A frittata, sliced tomatoes from the garden, a salad of bitter, dandelion-like greens, wine. With his fingers Maurizio sprinkled salt over my food until I said, *basta*.

3. On the same trip at another villa my cousin Giorgio, seated outdoors behind a palazzo on a promontory overlooking Portofino, takes a ripe peach from a bowl at the center of the table. Using his pocketknife he peels off the skin, slices the peach into segments, dropping them one by one into his dish. Evening, and the lights are fine in a distance far across the black water. Someone passes him the wine, chilled and white, with which he drowns the fruit saying, with his mouth full, in English: dessert.

How to Eat a Pet
A Gastronomic Adventure in the Andes

by Lynn Levin

I have been known to eat foods that others snub. As a student, I lived off back-of-the-store, reduced-price vegetables and fruits. Day-or-more-old muffins and Danish were a treat. My best company dish was a cheap and tasty enchilada casserole that I made with chicken necks and backs. So it was only natural I should one day undertake a real gastronomic adventure. I should try to eat a pet, a nice small one. A guinea pig would do, and the place to accomplish that was Peru, where *cuy*, as guinea pig is known, was said to be a staple of the traditional diet.

Of course, I didn't travel to Peru just to challenge the frontiers of dining. It had long been my dream to explore the cloud-crested ruins of Machu Picchu and to glide upon Lake Titicaca in a reed boat. I wanted to brush up on my Spanish. I wanted to experience the Andes. I wanted to try a dish so repellent that I could brag about it for the rest of my life. No matter that the furry beasts were the hapless servants of science, or that my sister and I once kept them as pets, or that every single person I spoke to curled his face in revulsion when I announced my intention to dine on a creature normally at home on a bed of cedar shavings. The more folks made retching motions, the more I rubbed my palms together with anticipation over a dish of something I imagined as a kind of mammalian Cornish game hen. I pledged to myself that I would consume *cuy* and then return home to triumphantly proclaim to my sister that *I had eaten Fluffy*.

How fondly I remembered my sister Judy's sweet-tempered little calico guinea pig. Fluffy loved to be held and stroked. We had tea parties for her. We made her salads with tough outer lettuce leaves. Fluffy nibbled on carrot tops and rabbit pellets. She didn't exercise much, but neither did anyone in our family. She lounged through a placid life until we felt she needed a mate and introduced Mickey into her cage. A hefty albino, Mickey had beady red eyes, a nasty attitude, and a pair of tusks that drew more than their share of our blood.

The match, I think, was a cruel one. I have often regretted it. Therefore it would have been more fitting to imagine myself biting into the hostile Mickey in retribution. But I imagined him as bitter and tough. There would be no pleasure in his degustation, none of the delight of eating Fluffy.

In Peru, I learned that *cuy* was prepared in a number of ways. You could make it stuffed and roasted, piquant and quartered, or flattened whole and fried. And while my host family in Cusco, the Mariscals, never served it at *almuerzo*, our main midday meal, *cuy* is said to be widely consumed in Peru. According to the author of *Unmentionable Cuisine*, veterinarian and food expert Calvin Schwabe, *cuy* provides over 50 percent of Peru's animal protein. Many people raise guinea pigs at home, and others buy them killed and cleaned in the meat section of the market. Ask a Peruvian if he or she eats *cuy*, and you will hear that person wax sentimental about the way his or her mamá prepared it—the same way an American will rhapsodize about Mom's apple pie or fried chicken. Still, as much as the Peruvians boasted of their favorite *cuy* fricassee or roast *cuy*, not once did I see an Andean or a Criollo actually eat *cuy*.

So why should my mind and guts rebel before a carefully prepared dish of pet? Was I just too ethnocentric? Did I think it barbaric or taboo? If I were starving, I would probably see things differently.

Cuy is by no means the most stomach-turning thing one can consume. In some parts of the Amazon jungle, people eat monkey, an animal whose genome is too close to human for my taste. Apropos of the human genome, food writer Jen Karetnick, who has done considerable research on Peruvian witchcraft, reveals that in some remote areas of Peru certain cooks may stir stew with a human femur or scrape bits of skull into a marinade of fish. Karetnick explains that this is part of a spell-casting ritual, adding that the use of human remains in cooking is strictly illegal in Peru. Good to hear that, since fish with skull is another no-brainer for me. But in the Andes what did I eat unawares? There's a mystery.

The issue of cannibalism or quasi-cannibalism aside, food tastes and food taboos are relative. The Chinese eat cat and dog. Moses declared that locusts were kosher. The Japanese challenge death by indulging in the poisonous *fugu* fish. The Philippinos drink and chew the delicacy of *balut*, the nearly mature embryo of a chick cooked in its shell. And what about haggis, the stuffed sheep's stomach so dear to Scottish palates and my own? I did not want to be ethnocentric. I wanted to overcome a food prejudice and eat a pet, a pet that, unfortunately, also happened to be a rat.

Rodent eating, however, is not unheard of even in America. Squirrel is a classic ingredient in Brunswick stew. In some parts of New Jersey, fire companies and churches hold muskrat dinners. On the Internet, you can find recipes for muskrat, or marsh hare, as it is sometimes known. I also found a recipe for Rottweiler with sweet potatoes. But I digress. The Peruvians think it bizarre and hilarious that Americans keep guinea pigs as pets.

For the first two weeks in Peru I demurred when it came to *cuy*. I dined on *ají gallina*, a spicy chicken stew, and *lomo saltado*, a yummy stir-fried beef dish gilded with French fries. I particularly liked alpaca, a meat which I found a little chewy, but very tasty. Grilled and attractively plated, it looked just like scallops of beef. At almost every meal I ate *choclo*, the bland, starchy, mega-kernelled corn that is a staple of the Peruvian diet. It didn't taste as good as it looked, but served with a chunk of salty cheese—a bite of *choclo*, a bite of *queso*—I learned to like it better. I developed a fondness for *mana*, a kind of giant marshmallow-sized sweetened popcorn, a popular snack you could buy from street vendors. Peru, of course, is the birthplace of corn and potatoes, and one is served spuds of all types: yellow, white, purple—dried and reconstituted, and then some.

It was not until I was in the town of Aguas Calientes, a maze of repetitive souvenir shops, restaurants, and hostels that served the budget tourists to Machu Picchu that I bellied up to the challenge of eating guinea pig. It was now or never, I thought, for after Machu Picchu I would journey on to Lake Titicaca, and I didn't know if I would be able to order *cuy* there.

This was February, the height of the rainy season. In Aguas Calientes, torrents Niagara'd off the awnings of the shops and restaurants. Deluges turned the staircase-like streets into tributaries of the Urubamba, the river that roared and rushed through the town and by the base of Machu Picchu. The town itself is called "Hot Waters" after its thermal springs, popular with the younger hikers. While my traveling partners, Michelle and Nancy, dared the spa, I passed, being fastidious, if not about eating strange things, then at least about stewing in a pool of backpacker bacteria. The rain had put a damper on our spirits. We did not look forward to hiking the ruins during a downpour, but magically the skies cleared the morning we were to visit Machu Picchu, and I even saw a flock of green parrots wing by a mountainside.

Never discovered, hence never destroyed by the Spaniards, Machu Picchu stands in silent majesty along the eyebrow of the rainforest. We spent a glorious morning exploring its emerald agricultural terraces and its common, royal, and sacred precincts, a sublime and strenuous visit. By the time we returned to Aguas Calientes we had worked up an appetite. It was time for my next adventure. It was time to try *cuy*.

Together we searched for a suitable restaurant. We dismissed quite a few: too expensive, too pretentious, not clean, no guinea pig, overly expensive guinea pig. At last we settled on a homey little place called El Candamo, mostly because of its comically mistranslated menu, which was headlined: "Plates to the pleasure give the victim."

Here, the Roasted Alpaca or *Asado de Alpaca* was known as Roasted He/She Gives German Nickel. Trout Roman-style or *Trucha a la Romana* was Trout to the Roman One. *Milanesa de Pollo* or Chicken Milanese-style became Milanesa Gives Chicken. Then there was my favorite: *Milanesa a la Napolitana de Res* or Milanesa to the Neapolitan One Gives Head. Michelle ordered trout. Nancy asked for spaghetti. Though I regretted having to pass up that Milanese and Neapolitan combo, I went for the *Cuy al Horno*: oven-roasted *cuy*. It cost thirty-two soles or about ten dollars, and I watched with some trepidation as the cook took the small, prepared mammal, laid it on a shallow white tray, and slid it into a wood-burning clay oven. Soon after I finished my *Cusqueña* beer, the dish was ready. The waitress smiled at me ironically.

Fluffy lay on the plate congealed and scorched, paws up, claws and head on, ringed with *papas fritas*, a huge log of *choclo*, and a few slices of cucumber and tomato. The garnishes surrounded her the way flowers garland the body at a funeral parlor. Fluffy was helpless. Her hind legs were splayed in indignity. Her orifices winked at me. Lest one take her for a pig, her two pairs of chisel-like incisors classed her at once in the order *Rodentia*. Fluffy had bits of herb over her eyes. Her mouth was frozen into an unmerry rictus, that sarcastic grin born by Death, who always has the last laugh. "So, living stiff," she chortled silently, "eat me. I dare you."

The body of the *cuy* was pierced at various points to let the fat run out. With much difficulty I split it open with the dull table knife. Inside was a dark green stuffing, made mostly of parsley and flavored with various herbs. It was potent and aromatic, but as I dipped in a second time, I came up with a fork of noodle-like stuff; the animal's intestines were mixed in with the green. So much for the stuffing. I took a deep breath for courage then cut and mostly combed at the meat with my fork. It was a labor-intensive dish. I found I had to separate the thin sheets of meat from the leather and subcutaneous fat. After giving Michelle and Nancy as much as they would accept—about two teaspoons each—I tried the meat. It was pungent, perhaps from the herb stuffing. There was a slipperiness to it. It was stringy and chewy and tasted like pork. And that was enough *cuy* for me.

Partly out of respect for my companions, partly out of respect for the corpse, I drew some tiny flimsy restaurant napkins over Fluffy's face and body. Thankfully Nancy was generous in sharing her spaghetti, and Michelle gave me some of her guacamole. The *Cusqueña* helped. All that plus a serious loss of appetite made for an adequate lunch.

My friend, Odi Gonzales, who is not only a noted Peruvian poet but also a genuine ethnic Inca with a passion for *cuy*, later told me that you are supposed to pick up the *cuy* whole with your hands and suck the meat off the thin bones. You then draw out and discard any bones that end up in your mouth. Clearly my knifing and forking had not contributed positively to my rodent-eating experience. I thought of the waitress at El Candamo and her sly smile. It must have been routinely funny to see the tourists struggle with the varmint. In her heart I think she knew that I would have been better off with the Milanesa to the Neapolitan One Gives Head.

Those of us who are not vegetarians eat dead things. This is a common fact. If you accept that humans are omnivores, which I do, we as a species kill and cook so that we may eat and live. I have never had much patience for sanctimonious vegetarians who tell me that morally I should be able to kill a cow if I want the right to eat steak. Nevertheless, there is something shocking about the frankness of seeing the cooked body intact. Of seeing the thing with its teeth. Many people, said Dr. Schwabe, have a bias against eating an animal served whole. Some will not eat fish with the head on, or roast suckling pig.

Well, it was that, of course, but it was also that the darn thing was a rat. As far as the gastronomy of disgust goes, I'd give whole, roasted guinea pig at least an eight. So when it came time to report to my sister about eating Fluffy, I had to confess that I had eaten her, but not very much.

On the other hand, I obtained a new degree of self-knowledge. I discovered that when it came to eating strange things, I was not as brave as I thought. Some might even call me chicken.

If you, too, wish to overcome a food prejudice and eat a pet, you may want to know how to prepare *cuy*. I came across this recipe in Peru.

Recipe for Stuffed Guinea Pig

YOU WILL NEED:
one clean guinea pig
onion
ground chili pepper and ground red chili pepper (both very spicy)
cooking oil
parsley
oregano
mint
huacatay (an herb that tastes and smells like a blend of black mint and marigold)
walnuts
salt
butter

The recipe, obviously not one for the beginning cook, instructs you to open the guinea pig ventrally, then to salt and drain it. After salting and draining, remove the organs and intestines, but do not wash the *cuy* anymore. Parboil the innards separately, then pierce them and dress them with onion, chili pepper, and oil. In another container, prepare a finely chopped mixture of the parsley, mint, oregano, *huacatay*, walnuts, and salt. Combine the mixture with the cooked organs and intestines and stuff all that back into the body cavity of the guinea pig. Coat the guinea pig with butter and ground red pepper. Place the critter in a roasting pan and cook it in the oven "until it's done."

Revised American instructions: First, go to a pet store....

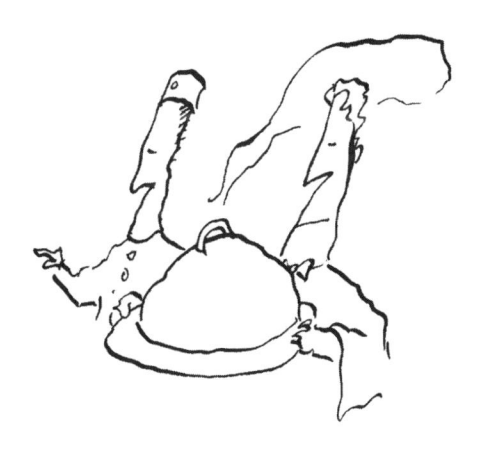

The Twelve-Course Dinner of Regret
by Terri Brandmueller

In a country where tumblers
of scotch and VSOP brandy are
drunk with dinner
like water I sit shoeless

with the cousin of the king
in a seaside town
on the Gulf of Siam

while the locals pay homage
with dried fish
and vintage *nam pla*

Prince Tanadsri
savors the fish sauce like fine wine
while the sun burns another
hole in the *Haw Mok*

the plates pile up
and an intoxicating fog of
lemongrass, cilantro and pandanus

makes me forget why I'm
not wearing shoes
the only thing that keeps my head
out of the *Tom Yam Goong*
is the fisheye

of the Prince's assistant,
and a strange voice in my ear assuring me of
the superior hygienic standards of the
Thai food processing industry

I have a vague idea that someone
has stolen my shoes
the waiter brings
more food and more scotch

until at last there is something that could be
dessert

back in the air-conditioned Mercedes
I'm relieved to see my shoes
have reappeared
on my feet

but as the chauffeur pulls the car
out into the stormy sea of traffic
back to Bangkok

I sink into the cool leather
looking for a place to throw-up
what may have been
the best meal of my life

What We Bring to the Table
by Margaret MacInnis

2005. My father went first. His mother, my grandmother, followed close behind. It was too much for Nanni, burying another child. Before I was born, when my father was a boy of sixteen, my grandmother lost her eighteen-year-old daughter, my namesake, in a freak car accident. Although I did not know the first Margaret, I am reminded of her each time I write or speak or hear my name. The doctor said my grandmother died of a broken heart and not the Easter egg of a lump on her head she asked me to touch one afternoon. We had been sitting at the table in her small, dark kitchen when she lowered her chin to her chest and took my hand, guiding it to the lump hidden beneath her set and dyed hair. I bumped my head, she said, and she had, but the lump was cancer. A few months later she was gone. My grandfather followed, his arteries clogged with nicotine, fried steak, and vodka. And after my grandfather, my maternal Nana died. She did, however, wait until I had married. Yes, I had a husband, but he's gone too, gone to that place where ex-husbands go. You cannot get there from here. Along with my husband went my mother-in-law and her complicated love. What remains is a water stain of memories, a delicate imprint that darkens with time.

2003. I am alone but not alone. I have Aunt Mary. Ninety-one-year-old Aunt Mary is not my aunt at all, and growing up I knew her only from St. Denis Catholic Church. In the three years since my separation, my return home, and my divorce, Mary and I have become friends. One afternoon she leads me through her kitchen to the dining room. She points to the table and tells me to sit. In the center sits an electric skillet full of homemade tomato sauce, sweet Italian sausage, and plump meatballs. Next to it is an opened bottle of red table wine. She spreads a hand-woven placemat in front of me before she brings me a plate, exactly as my grandmother Nanni, Mary's first cousin, would have done.

Mary's mother and my great-grandfather, Nanni's father, were Savianos, brother and sister, Italian immigrants from Pomigliano d'Arco, a small, impoverished city in the Campania region. Somehow they found their way to the axe and woolen mills of Douglas, Massachusetts, where they married other Italian immigrants and between the two of them, raised eighteen children, whose children and, grandchildren would also build lives in Douglas. I am one of the few who went away, first to college and then overseas to teach. That I found my way home still surprises me.

Mary tells me to help myself, and just for me, she says, she has put a surprise in the meatballs. Raisins, just like your grandmother. The traditional Saviano family recipe for meatballs called for raisins, Mary explains, but because her brothers didn't like raisins, her mother made their meatballs without. Her cousins, my grandmother included, kept the raisins. Upon Mary's instruction I pour wine into water glasses. Just a splash for me, she says. When I clink my raised glass to hers, she says, To life.

꧁꧂

2000. At four in the morning, while my husband and house guests sleep, I pour a cup of coffee at the kitchen table, which is tucked under the window against the wall. On a good day I would call this kitchen space cozy, and on a bad day, cramped. But I live and teach in Villars-sur-Ollon, Switzerland, and the way the green mountains grow up from the valley, higher and higher until the white peaks rise past my windows and meet the sky, more than compensates for lack of counter space. These snowy mountain views, unfortunately, do not compensate for lack of respect and loss of desire, not even at sunset. Love, I have learned, can die in the most beautiful places. I wrap both hands tightly around my coffee cup. I know what I have to do. I drink the last of my coffee and release the cup from my grip. On a page torn out of my journal, I begin a letter goodbye.

☙

2000. As the first day of our two day trip to Aosta, Italy, closes, my husband, mother, sister, and brother-in-law gather around a table in the crowded Ristorante Moderno. Tourist trap, my husband says, even though the dining room tables spill over with Italians. He hates tourists, and he hates Aosta, he told me when I said I wanted to visit with my family. He does not want to be here. A TV hangs over our table, and my husband fixes his eyes on the soccer match above my head, pulling them away only to roll them as the rest of us pass our plates around, sampling our different pasta selections—pesto, marinara, four cheese, garlic and oil, and hot red pepper sauce. I try to concentrate on the food, the wine, and the laughter, but my husband's mood weighs me down like a small lead weight tied to a balloon.

☙

1999. My Ukrainian mother-in-law, born in Lvov when it belonged to Poland and later married to a Jewish man who took her and her son to Canada, comes to visit us and stays for three weeks at a time. I don't mind, I tell her, and part of me means it. I enjoy her company, the way she throws open a window to my husband's past. I happily eat the food of my husband's youth, the *pierogis* she calls *varenkis*, *galumpkis*, the deep purple borcht, and the chicken bouillon, as if by eating it I will know him better. My mother-in-law will stock the freezer with more of this food before she leaves. Later I will defrost it, imagining her as a girl in Poland before it became Ukraine. I will imagine her chubby and pink-cheeked, clutching poppy stems. I will imagine her before her life changed, before a neighbor found her father, a Polish nationalist, in a field, shot dead, a bullet between his eyes and one through his heart. I will imagine my mother-in-law before she ate soup made from boiled weeds, before she grew lean and hard, and I will love her.

☙

My husband and I don't have an ironing board, which dismays my mother-in-law, who has spent over three decades ironing clothes for her husband and sons. A daughter to help would have been nice. Instead she got me, the American woman in the wrinkled shirt. After our breakfast of white bread, butter, caviar, and coffee, she clears the dishes. There is work to be done. She spreads a towel across the kitchen table and plugs in the iron. Her son needs pressed shirts. As I head out the door, she, matador-fashion, snaps open a cotton shirt and sighs; in her snap and sigh, I hear disappointment.

Late one morning, my mother-in-law watches me lean against the wall and slide down into a crouched position. I know how to cook, Irina. Let me cook tonight.

She nods, allowing me back into my kitchen. While I cook, she and my husband will drive into the valley. As soon as they leave, I begin chopping tomatoes, fresh basil, onions, and garlic for sauce. To make meatballs, I drop raw ground beef, pork, and an egg into a bowl, add salt, pepper, and oregano, and knead the ingredients with my hands until the mixture is blended. While the sauce simmers, I roll the meatballs, feeling a pang of guilt for forgetting to buy the raisins. I grate fresh *parmigiano*, bought in Aosta, and cut what remains of the morning's baguette. The smell of the sauce fills the kitchen, wafting down the hallway, seeping into every corner of our apartment under the eaves. We will, I have decided, eat at the table in the living room rather than in the kitchen. Feeling content, I set this table, light two candles, and open a bottle of red.

When my husband and Irina walk through the door with arms full of grocery bags, my husband says, oh, honey, the smells, the smells. Food compliments come easy to him as they did to my grandfather, who never held back at the end of a meal: Thanks, Rosie. That was damn good. He might not have spoken to my grandmother all morning or afternoon, he might have eaten his meal in silence, he might have been too drunk on screwdrivers to find his way home the previous night, but he always complimented her cooking.

Doesn't it smell good, Mama?

Irina nods. It's the garlic. Nice, Maggie.

Maggie? I did not ask her to call me Maggie. When did she start?

After she and my husband put away the groceries, I tell them to go and sit at the table in the living room. I will serve them. My husband pours wine into the crystal goblets we received as wedding gifts five years ago. Just a little sauce for me, Irina says, taking the ladle for the sauce from my hand. She serves herself one meatball and spoons one dollop of sauce onto her spaghetti. I don't like tomato sauce, Maggie.

1998. One morning in Kuwait, my husband throws his coffee cup at me. I see it coming and move before it hits me. When I see my grandfather in his eyes, I have to look away. Pick it up, he says, and (it pains me now to admit) I do.

1997. It is New Year's Eve in the ski resort town of Chamonix, France. My husband and I have come from Kuwait for winter vacation to get our fill of red wine and alpine runs. This night we sit in a crowded bar at a table with strangers. He glances at me before he reaches for a pitcher of beer. Angry over our most recent squabble over where we will be next year, I sit with my arms crossed. Lighten up, he says, and I look away. The band plays so loudly that I cannot make out the words of the song. As he chugs his beer, I would like to tell him: The walls are closing in. Instead I tell him that I need to find the restroom. I think I'm actually going there. But when I see the side exit door cracked open, I slip out into the chilly night. I run through the crowded streets back to our hotel room, crashing into a parked bicycle en route. I will have an ugly bruise, and my husband will not forgive me for abandoning him before midnight.

1995. On New Year's Eve my husband and I are alone at my mother's isolated mountain cabin. We have been married for a year and thirteen days. Depression like a blanket of snow has settled over me. I am praying for a thaw. When the electricity goes out at nine, I climb up to the loft to sleep. Just before midnight my husband wakes me. The lights are back on. I have a surprise, he says. Come on. He slaps my thigh. Get up.

 I follow him down the ladder and find the table set with a candle, a half empty bottle of vodka, two shot glasses, and on a large cracked plate I have not seen before, he has laid whatever he could find in the fridge and cupboards: pickles, cheddar, wheat crackers, and honey-roasted mixed nuts. His kind, simple gesture moves me, and I think that if we can string one kind, simple gesture after another, we can make a life together.

1995. Four months after my wedding, I telephone Nana, my mother's great-aunt, in the hospital. My mother answers the phone and hands it to Nana, who reassures me that she will not die until she has rocked her Maggie's babies. Although I cannot see babies in my future, I am her Maggie, and have been since she opened her home to my young parents. She tried to raise us all. That night, her heart, weakened by childhood polio, stops.

My husband covers my fifth grade language arts class and I fly home from England. After the funeral, I follow the others into the church basement, where the Bereavement Club has prepared food and coffee. I recognize Mary immediately, her features so distinctly Saviano that my eyes fill. She resembles my grandmother, her first cousin, but her kind, gentle smile reminds me of Nana. From behind a table covered with assorted cookies and freshly-baked loaves of nut, banana, and zucchini bread, Mary waves. Although I have not seen her in years, she holds out her arms to embrace me.

ə♥

1992. Val's kitchen smells like onion and garlic, and I open all the windows. My tomato sauce bubbles over like Vesuvio, and I hurry to clean the stovetop before he returns from his tennis match. We have been dating for a month, and this evening I'm cooking for him for the first time. I reduce the flame under the sauce and begin to grate cheese for a second dish. Val wants a cheese sauce too. I don't own a cookbook, so I'm experimenting with gorgonzola, parmigiano, and mozzarella. I hope it turns out all right. You just never know with such experiments. To ease my anxiety, I open a bottle of Turkish red and pour a glass. Closer to dinnertime I boil water for spaghetti and tortellini. I slice tomatoes and cucumbers and arrange them on a plate with Greek olives, but we live in Istanbul, so they are Turkish olives. I test the pasta, turn off the sauces, and wait. I drink another glass. I drink until the Turkish wine tastes Italian, and I am tipsy when I reheat the cold food, tipsy when we sit down to eat, tipsy when he takes a bite, tipsy when I wait for his reaction, and tipsy when he leans into me for a kiss.

ə♥

1992. Our first morning together, I walk into Val's kitchen and find the table spread with a breakfast of fresh Turkish bread, still warm from the bakery, butter, and an open jar of strawberry jam, a teaspoon resting in its upside-down cover. He has taken such care with the table that I smile from the deep place where woman-child Margaret-Maggie lives. He smiles back. I want this to be love. When he hands me a cup and saucer for my coffee, he smiles. How's my girl?

ਵ

1986. Home from college for the weekend, I walk through my grandmother's door. She points to the kitchen table. I've got a surprise for you. She spreads a hand-woven placemat in front of me and gives me the thin cotton vest I wear each time I eat with her. No stains for her granddaughter. I snap the vest closed. She opens the oven and bends to pull out a plate of gnocchi.

ਵ

1986. Sometimes I cannot believe I made it to college. I cannot believe many things, so I throw myself into art history and Italian language studies at Emmanuel College. During my first semester, at a restaurant in the North End of Boston, I eat gnocchi sorrentini for the first time. My grandmother, my Neapolitan Nanni, has never prepared the small potato dumplings in a light tomato and basil sauce. On my next visit to her house, as she stands at the stove frying steak and eggs for my grandfather's lunch, I ask why she never makes gnocchi. She looks at me. I've made her sad. My mother used to make them, she says. They're a lot of work. And the old man would never eat them.

The old man is my grandfather, and all I ever see him eat are cuts of meat and mashed potatoes, washed down, these days, with cold water. I would like to wrap my arms around her, but she would not like that. Instead I say: I'd eat your gnocchi, Nanni.

ਵ

1985. My father sits at the kitchen table in the apartment that he and I have shared since my parents' divorce. I am sixteen and out for the afternoon. I do not know that I will not see my father alive again after today. He writes on a yellow legal pad he has brought home from work. Margaret, never forget there wasn't a moment when I wasn't terribly proud of you. Ma and Dad, I'm sorry I caused you so much trouble. He reaches across the table for the rotary phone on the wall. He dials the police station and informs the dispatcher that John MacInnis has been shot. After he hangs up, he waits a minute, maybe two. He presses his handgun to his temple and fires one precise, fatal shot.

The policeman, who hears the shot as he is getting out of his car, is a friend and neighbor. When he kicks down the door, he finds my father on the floor beside the table.

ཞ

1985. My father and I are living together in half of a duplex on Main Street. Before he leaves to supervise the transition between second and third shifts at the Sweet Life, Quality Foods warehouse, he makes a pot of coffee. You really shouldn't be drinking coffee this late, he says, pouring me a cup. We sit at the table with our coffee. He takes a long drag from his cigarette. You need to know something, he says. I put my cup down. He tells me this: The walls are closing in. I reach for my cup, wrapping both hands tightly around it, imagining I have the power to hold our life together.

ཞ

1983. My father has left. This time my mother asked him to. He has moved into a cramped apartment on North Street, but he comes, dressed in black from his sweater to his leather boots, to watch us open our Christmas presents. As my mother pours him a cup of fresh coffee, she asks how he wants his eggs.

At the mention of food, he shakes his head, curling his lip in disgust. He can't eat.

You have to eat, my mother says. You're skin and bones.

He cradles his stomach and rocks. I can't. My ulcer's killing me.

My mother disappears into the bathroom and comes out with something he forgot to take when he left, his bottle of Mylanta. She places it on the table in front of him. Drink some now. I'll get a spoon.

He unscrews the cap and swigs from the bottle.

Over easy, he says. My mother looks confused. The eggs. I'll take them over easy.

1980. My father has become a supervisor and works second shift. My mother feeds me and sends me to bed long before he comes home. Even though my father is sober now, I cannot sleep until he walks through the door. Awake in my bed, I listen to my mother open and close kitchen drawers and cupboards. She begins with potatoes. He wants them every night, but she can't stand to peel them. She makes them from a box of dried flakes that she keeps hidden behind the Tupperware. I hear a sizzle as my mother places my father's steak in a frying pan of melted butter. Next she opens and drains a tin of Sweet Life mushrooms, and dumps them into the pan. The aroma wafts into my bedroom and my stomach aches with what might be hunger.

1979. Sunday dinner is the only time we eat together and almost every Sunday we eat real potatoes and the roast beef dinner my mother's great-aunt has prepared. Nana (not Nanni) lets us live in her house without paying rent, so my mother buys the roast beef and peels the potatoes. My father sits at one end of the table and Nana sits at the other. We take turns saying grace.

1978. On Thanksgiving we eat with Nanni and Puppa, my father's parents; my father has stopped drinking, and he sits on the couch, smoking and staring at the TV. Puppa, also smoking and staring at the TV, is drinking a screwdriver. Nanni and my mother are in the kitchen getting dinner ready. They whisper when they speak, my mother's voice urgent, and my grandmother's voice growing louder and louder, until her *Love him? I don't love him. I hope he drinks himself to death* fills the living room. The words sting my eyes like cigarette smoke. My father pales, my grandfather clears his throat, and I pretend to be reading Soap Opera Digest.

 Later, we sit around the table as if nothing was said. When my grandfather finishes his meal, he stands and says what he says at the end of every holiday meal, Thank you, Rosie. That was damn good.

ð

1978. At St. Denis Catholic Church, I sit in a pew alongside my family, waiting for my favorite part of the Mass—Holy Communion. Today is a special day, my father explained earlier this morning. Communion has changed. If I want to, when I go up to the altar to take communion, instead of sticking out my tongue and waiting for the priest to place the host on it, I can hold out my cupped hands to receive the body of Christ, the bread of life. Only if I want to, my father said.

I want to, I said, and he asked why.

Because I want to hold Jesus in my hands.

My father does not know if it is right, but I can do what I want. I fidget in the pew. I cannot wait. When it is time to go to the altar, I am first. I hold out my hands to the silver-haired priest. I smile a wide, gleeful smile, and he has to smile back, a tight flash of a smile, but still a smile. I say amen, put the host in my mouth, make the sign of the cross, and turn to see my father holding out his hands.

ð

1975. Saturday evening means homemade baked beans, salt pork, and corn bread with butter. Nana instructs me to set the table. We are alone. My father has to attend ninety meetings in ninety days and my mother goes with him to make sure he gets there. Nana opens the oven, and wearing my mother's oven mitts, I remove the pot of beans as I do every Saturday. And like every Saturday the warm, sweet aroma of the baked beans stirs me. Just last night these same beans, pale and hard, were soaking on the counter in a pan full of water. The small transformation sustains me.

ð

1971. I sit at the head of a toddler-sized wooden table that someone has assembled in the corner of the kitchen. My eyes fix on the tall figure at the stove. I am close enough to reach out and touch his leg. I could squeeze the soft denim of his fading jeans in my fist and hold on tight. But I sit with my hands folded on the table in front of me, gazing up at my father. Honey, I hope you're hungry.

He puts a bowl of soup in front of me. Mmm. Cream of Mushroom. It's good. Let it cool first. In the middle of my table, he places a grilled cheese sandwich, which isn't grilled at all, but pan-fried in butter. My father, holding a knife and the butter dish, kneels down on the floor next to me. It's better this way, he says, spreading my sandwich with more butter. I watch it melt. Then he cuts the sandwich in two diagonally. When I reach for a half, he taps my hand. Eat your soup first, he says, but I don't like the color or the smell of the soup. Nana makes me tomato, but she has gone grocery shopping with my mother. He picks up my spoon and stirs the soup with it. Then he holds a spoonful to his mouth and blows. He feeds me. The soup doesn't taste bad or good, but my father has made it. He watches me, waiting for my reaction, so I smile and tell him it's good. That's my girl. You do it yourself now. When he hands me the spoon, I hold it tightly, slowly empting my bowl, one spoonful at a time.

Tomato Love
by C. Kevin Smith

The tomato arrived in a small, brown cardboard box, wrapped in plain white paper. There was no note, only the familiar handwriting on the box: from my father, to me. He had begun planting tomatoes again, and this one, he knew, was one of the season's best.

My father grew up in rural Missouri during the Depression. Missouri soil is famously fertile, which was a good thing for my father's family, because sometimes the only thing to eat was whatever they could grow. Now, years later, after divorce and relocation, retirement and a period of unsettled confusion, he had planted tomatoes in the tiny yard next to his trailer, in Santa Monica. He also tended to some tomato plants a few blocks away, belonging to a ninety-year-old woman he had met at the local senior's center.

He would speak to me of these tomatoes, on the phone and in letters, marking their passage from seed to bud, from fruit to supper, his words expressing a quiet, confident satisfaction. The world might go to hell, but with proper care a beautiful tomato could be cultivated and enjoyed. He and I were past the phase of mutual bewilderment and suspicion that had begun in my teens and lasted a decade or so, and I appreciated these conversations. He might feel lonely at times; his tomatoes, at least, still needed him.

I opened the box and took out the tomato. I knew this was a prize specimen: smooth, unblemished skin, stretched taut over flesh that yielded but was not too soft, its deep, red color promising pleasure. It smelled powerfully of sweetness and tang, sunlight and dirt. I felt a curious mixture of tickled delight and worried awe for what my father had done, sending a single ripe tomato via the U.S. Mail—astonishment, too, that it had traveled hundreds of miles without acquiring the slightest bruise or tear.

It was a large tomato. I held it in one hand, its base easily covering my palm, and felt the heaviness of its juices. I set it on the kitchen counter to let it rest after its journey. I wanted to eat it at just the right time.

In the 1970s, my father became interested in organic gardening, but I don't recall him growing tomatoes. Corn, squash, green beans, chard, also a brief period devoted to fruit trees. I haven't asked him about this, but I think his current involvement with tomatoes has something to do with his Missouri boyhood, some seed of his life then, perhaps long forgotten, now once again bearing fruit. To be a grower of tomatoes one must have considerable skill, knowledge, sensitivity to the elements, patience. But to produce a tomato that is truly great, one must have something else: an intuitive attachment to the soil, a sixth sense of what makes things live. Children, who are by necessity close to the ground, often have this kind of understanding, or belief. But as we grow and take on responsibilities this connection is easily lost.

There is one other important ingredient in the creation of a successful tomato. It is love. This is what I tasted in abundance as I held my head over the kitchen sink, some hours after the tomato's arrival, when I could stand to wait no longer. I bit into the fruit of my father's labor, sweet and sharp, and felt a burst of gratitude to have a father who always did, and would still, provide.

Tomato Garden
by Kerry Trautman

Learning nature's order of light and water,
I gardened my first home.
Didn't weed or water enough, but nonetheless
a tomato plant grew. It forgave me.

And when that first fruit swelled
green to gold to rust to red,
I plucked, and smelled its dirty sun warmth,
already feeling the acid sweet on my tongue,
stinging a tiny cut on my lip.

I sliced the skin, arranged brilliant
red wedges on a green-and-blue-rimmed plate,
pinched the slightest of Kosher salt,
fresh-cracked black pepper,
bent my face to the plate and inhaled
the luminous wet tang of summer.

As I raised the first wedge to my lips,
I saw, in the pink flesh, a tiny worm,
mucously translucent and gold
curled still in his juicy home.

I forgave my tomato and ate the wedge
despite its worm, never tasting him,
so infused was he with juice,
so resigned was he to my tongue.

Recipe for Tomato Cabal
by Angus Woodward

How did the tomato come to be known
as the only vegetable which is actually
a fruit? Is there some shadowy trilateral
tomato commission in charge of this apotheosis?
Perhaps the same folks who centuries ago
promulgated the love-apple as the perfect
nontoxic basis for myriad sauces? I am
here to spread the word that while the tomato
is indeed a fruit, so is the cucumber,
as are zucchini, acorn, yellow, spaghetti,
and summer squashes. Spaghetti is not
a fruit—pay attention. Olives are just
as fruity as cherries and plums. Okra?
A fruit. Eggplant? Fruit, as are all peppers.
But why the obsession with fruitiness?
No one pipes up to say *the artichoke
is actually a flower!* Nobody points out
that lettuces are leaves, celery
mere stems, carrots roots. In being
actually a fruit, the tomato is nothing
special, my friends. And all this time,
false fruits have wandered the earth
undetected, unremarked. Sorry
to spring it on you so suddenly, but
sugar-sweet plant products
which are not fruit at all populate
your Frigidaires. Impostors.

I would tell you their names, but
I'd prefer not to stoop to the level
to which those shadowy tomato
public relations men have stooped.

Pears
by REAMY JANSEN

Today I bought pears here in Wadena to begin my residence as a visiting writer. My host, Kent Sheer, drove me to the Wadena True Value, where he tried to entice me into buying "our" (a.k.a., central Minnesota's) turkey and wild rice sausage. But I would have none of gizzards and grain. Instead, I headed off for the fruit section.

Coming from a tree whose genus is *Pyrus communis*, a pear or two was what I, a new arrival, craved. I don't know the many varieties of this fruit and can only conjure a few names: Anjou, Bartlett, Seckel; that's pretty much it. The three I bought were a speckled yellow brown silting into a fading green, a muted blend that I hoped carried my pear closer toward ripeness.

I'm not a good judge of a pear's freshness; they're hardly as simple as apples which, if firm, you pick one up and bite in. The solidity and shape of pears don't give them the lightness and evenly distributed weight of apples. Pears are compact and hard, hard as rocks sometimes, dense with gravity. I tried to pick up some with a bit of give, but this tenderness was deceptive, for when I bit into one at home, it was hard as a rock. I let the second selection sleep undisturbed for two days and then sliced into it the way my father did—part of his politesse with fruit—cutting, not biting. When I was a teen in the living room reading, he'd bring me six even sections on a plate.

This second pear was excellent.

My dad loved a bit of fruit, savored the juices, the entire act of preparing, serving, and eating, offices hinting at the sensuousness behind his solid, Republican persona, one fundamentally jolly and good-natured, and which I seem to have inherited, along with a jigger of my mother's madness. Pears, cherries, red grapes, and peaches—the runny fruits were his favorites. Was it this physicality my mother desired to avoid by going to bed later than he? Perhaps the juniper in gin may be considered fruit, for, as Spenser tells us, "Sweet is the Lunipere." My mother would stay on in the living room reading, as my father would head upstairs, his hand lightly gracing the polished mahogany banister. Certainly I possess his taste-in-touch.

When he was in his seventies and living alone in too large a house, I would bring him cherries, Bings, and laugh at his standing joke about Crosby not fitting into the bag. And when we would shop together he would buy pears, which he could hardly see but knew well by hand through his tapering, papery fingers.

Whenever I'm away somewhere writing, like now, with my studio in the town's assisted living center, The Pines, filled with a number of widowers like my dad once was, I buy a few pears. I have a shyness about buying them, and linger before their open baskets, never quite able to remember how to choose. Since I like both the idea of pearness and something of the thing itself, too, I just choose by color, usually reds or yellows, the color of maple leaves in the fall. I handle each pear carefully, though I learn little from doing this. Each day, I'll gently test the taut middle of my chosen pears. They are usually perfection a day or two later. Each swelling side makes way for my father's pen knife, his still-sharp blade easing through the grainy flesh, making thin, even slices, leaving a square core behind. I eat the gleaming pieces slowly, wetting my fingers.

At home, my wife, Leslie, who wants to give me all things, will sometimes buy me pears knowing that they mean something—what some people, perhaps the French, like to call the presence of absence. Knowing the nurturing lore of her grandparents' Maryland farm, she puts them in a paper bag, sure that this is how they will ripen. And they do.

Bartlett
by Jamie Granger

B
 a
  r
   t
    l
     e
      t
       t
All these
poems are
starting to look
like pears to me.
They're so slender
and shy when they begin,
mere wisps of ideas, hardly
willing to make an untoward
comment, overly polite, surprised,
even, that someone might read past
the ninth line where with, is it gravity,
or the ability to reproduce a whole tree
(and a thousand pears besides), they curve
voluptuously outward giving away the secret
of their seeds hidden deep inside soft pear
flesh. And just like those you buy in the
produce section at the grocery store, I
can almost see a tiny label — is it a
warning or an invitation — that
tells me, "Ripe when yields
to gentle pressure."

Let's Go Hog-Wild with Our Peaches!
by Anthony Russell White

Let's Go Hog-Wild with Our Peaches!
Fragment from a Broadway musical, set in rural Georgia. Our hero sings to his sweetheart, with help from the rest of the picking crew:

Just like we do each June,
singin' that fresh peach tune:
Dice'em in the pancakes, shortcakes!
Chop'em on the cornflakes, milkshakes!
Slice'em on the noodles! Serve'em to your poodles!
Don't scream, dream on—bury'em in the ice cream!
Every hand reaches—do we have enough peaches?

Escape From the Fat Farm
by Sandy McIntosh

DAY 1: "Cappy," our dining room host, announces: "You'll be served delightful low-calorie meals, and you *shall* lose weight!"

DAY 2: I gaze at my plate. The solitary pea that was on the edge has rolled over the rim and disappeared.

DAY 3: Cappy says beware the alligators in the moat. And keep hands off the rabbits. Delectable, yet their bites are deadly.

DAY 4: The table talk has turned entirely to food—if at breakfast, then about lunch. If at lunch, then about dinner. Then breakfast again. We are insatiable in our talk about food!

DAY 5: We suspect Little Tubby Moran has caught and eaten a rabbit. Our jealousy knows no bounds.

DAY 6: We've been debating the best method for capturing an alligator. "Can you whistle and they come?" No. "Can you call them: 'Hey, alligator! Hey, alligator!'" No. "And would pan roasting be easier, or stuff it whole into the oven?" Probably neither. "I'd rather have the shoes, belts and handbags," observes adorable Penelope, but the rest of us know the truth. She'd wrestle an alligator to death, its fritters steaming in the sun, if they'd just let us out of this building.

DAY 7: Our conversations are now whispered because Cappy is watching and listening, his hands clanking metal ball bearings, like Captain Queeg. He is definitely suspicious of our whispering.

DAY 8: The meals get no better. A slight diversion: our waiter, a new daddy, shows off his infant child. This event leaves us quiet, meditative. Our tablemate, Dr. X, an admitted amateur torturer, opines that cleaning, cooking and eating a human infant is as simple as cooking a baby pig. We find this horrible and disgusting, and we tell him so. But this leads to speculation on where we might find a baby pig.

DAY 9: Cappy now appears each night dressed as a pirate, complete with wooden leg. He twirls his pirate's gun and reminds us by certain gestures that it's loaded.

DAY 10: Someone serves us the wrong dinner! The menu said Steak with Mashed Potatoes and a Chocolate Milkshake! But all we got was a plate of spoons! Not even a steak knife! Little Tubby Moran complains loudly, but answer gets he none.

DAY 11: We are served a bowl of murky soup made with moat water. An openly hostile Cappy commands: "Get in there with your spoons and row, you blackguards!" And he fires a warning shot across our bow. It is understood that we must now address him as "Captain."

DAY 12: Little Tubby Moran has disappeared. Nobody says it, but we're all thinking the same thing: *cannibalism*. Dr. X is missing, also.

DAY 13: There is open talk of mutiny. The captain has chained us to the deck. We're fed only low-fat yogurt with the occasional strawberry floating in it. But all we need is the opportunity and Cappy goes down. Then we'll row ourselves across the moat to freedom and a good brunch.

DAY 14: A terrible storm at sea. Cartons of croutons and little packets of mayonnaise float by, but always out of reach. Penelope says: "Let's see if we can swim as far as the kitchen. I'll get a decent meal if I have to kill someone!" We manage this, and are awed. Refrigerators, their shelves weighed down with food, loom. And there is something else. In the blackness a lone figures stands between us and our dinner. It is Cappy aiming his pistol. "I'll take care of this," Penelope hisses, darkly determined. "This night we eat!"

DAY 15: Morning sun and quiet sea. At last, it's all over. Cappy has vanished. The dining room doors have opened. We, tattered survivors, pull ourselves together. Outdoors, a bucolic scene: alligators dozing like armored cars on the moat banks; sounds of tiny sprockets turning inside the bodies of caterpillars. And as we're led to the scales, we discover to our delight that we have lost weight, exactly as advertised in their brochure, though it's mostly arms and legs.

Contributor's Notes

Elisa Albo was born in Havana and grew up eating fantastic Cuban, Spanish and Jewish food. Her work has appeared in journals and anthologies, including *Crab Orchard Review* and *Irrepressible Appetites*. A chapbook, *Passage to America*, is forthcoming from March Street Press. She teaches at Broward Community College in Ft. Lauderdale.

Michele Battiste, a recent graduate of Wichita State University, was the 2004 MFA Poetry Fellow. Her work has appeared in several literary magazines and she received a 2005 AWP Intros Award. Author of the chapbook *Mapping the Spaces Between* (Snark Publishing), she currently lives in New York City.

Patsy Anne Bickerstaff is a former president of the Virginia Writers' Club and an executive board member of The Poetry Society of Virginia. She has published poetry and articles in numerous publications. She and her late husband, Wilson Lee Seay, are the authors of *Alcohol-Free Entertaining*, (Betterway Publications, 1985) a mocktail recipe book, which was a *Better Homes & Gardens* book-of-the month choice.

Terri Brandmueller is a former newspaper editor and food writer who lives and writes poetry in Brooklyn, New York. She has an MA in Media Studies from The New School and is currently working on a book about internet genealogy and family secrets.

T.M. De Vos lives and works on the East Coast. Her poetry and fiction have appeared in *Washington Square*, *Small Spiral Notebook*, *Yuan Yang: A Journal of Hong Kong and International Writing*, *Pebble Lake Review*, and *The Global City Review*.

Ruth E. Dickey's poems have appeared in *The Baltimore Review*, *Colere*, *Kaliope*, *Paper Street*, *The Potomac Review*, *Slipstream*, *Sonora Review* and others, and her chapbook is forthcoming from Pudding House Press. She currently lives in Seattle, where she is the Executive Director of New Futures.

Jehanne Dubrow was born in Vicenza, Italy and grew up in Yugoslavia, Zaire, Poland, Belgium, Austria, and the United States. She is currently pursuing a PhD in creative writing at the University of Nebraska-Lincoln. Her work has appeared in *The Hudson Review*, *Poetry*, *Tikkun*, and *The New England Review*.

Margarita Engle is a botanist and the Cuban-American author of several novels, most recently *The Poet Slave of Cuba*, a biography in poems (Henry Holt & Co., April, 2006). Short works have appeared in *Atlanta Review*, *California Quarterly*, *Caribbean Writer*, and *Hawaii Pacific Review*. Awards include a Cintas Fellowship, a San Diego Book Award, and a 2005 Willow Review Poetry Award.

Jamie Granger's work has appeared in *Atlanta Review*, *Black Warrior Review*, *Exquisite Corpse*, *Gulf Stream*, *Madison Review*, *Quarter After Eight*, *Quick Fiction*, *Rhino*, and others, and has been featured on National Public Radio's "All Things Considered." He grew up in Montserrat, West Indies, and lives in South Florida.

Amy Halloran lives and eats in Troy, New York with her husband, two sons, and up to six chickens. She is working on stories short and long for people old and young, and an oral history of the neighborhood near her that was destroyed to make way for a bridge.

Ellen Herbert's fiction has been read on NPR's "The Sound of Writing" and been published in *First for Women*. Her essays have appeared or are forthcoming in *The Sonora Review* and *The Rambler*. She is an assistant professor of literature and languages at Marymount University.

Ann Hood is the author of 7 novels, including *Somewhere Off the Coast of Maine: a memoir*; *Do Not Go Gentle: My Search for Miracles in a Cynical Time*; and a collection of short stories, *An Ornithologist's Guide to Life*. Her essays and stories have appeared in *The New York Times*, *Tin House*, *More*, *Ladies Home Journal*, *Good Housekeeping*, and *Traveler*. She has won the Paul Bowles Prize for Short Fiction, an American Spiritual Writing Award, and two Pushcart Prizes. Her new novel, *The Knitting Circle*, will be published in January, 2007, by WW Norton.

Reamy Jansen is Professor of English and Humanities at SUNY Rockland and a Contributing Editor to *The Bloomsbury Review of Books*. Recent essays and poems have appeared in *LIT*, *Gargoyle*, *32 Poems*, *UnpleasantEventSchedule* and the on-line anthology, *Enskyment*. His chapbook, *My Drive, A Natural History*, was published by Finishing Line Press, 2004. www.reamyjansen.com

Persis M. Karim lives in Berkeley, California and teaches writing and literature at San Jose State University. She regularly fantasizes about sharing a meal with some of her favorite poets, Neruda, Rumi, and Garci Lorca. She's editor/contributor of the forthcoming *Let Me Tell You Where I've Been: New Writing by Women of the Iranian Diaspora* (2006) and co-editor of *A World Between: Poems, Short Stories and Essays by Iranian Americans* (1999).

Annie Kay is a Registered Dietitian, yoga instructor and health and medical writer living on Nantucket Island, MA and Kauai, HI with her husband Craig and her cat, Rahu. She is an avid cook, gardener, yogini, poet and outdoorswoman.

Lynn Levin is the author of two poetry collections, *Imaginarium* (Loonfeather Press, 2005) and *A Few Questions about Paradise* (Loonfeather Press, 2000). She teaches creative writing at the University of Pennsylvania and at Drexel University, where she is also executive producer of the cable TV show, *The Drexel InterView*.

Margaret MacInnis's work has appeared or is forthcoming in *Gettysburg Review, Louisville Review, Crab Orchard Review, Potomac Review, Brevity, Caketrain,* and *Literary Mama*. She is the recent winner of the *Literal Latte* Essay Contest, and a Virginia Center for the Creative Arts fellow. She holds an MFA from Queens University of Charlotte.

Sandy McIntosh once edited *Wok Talk*, the Chinese cooking journal. His books include *From A Chinese Kitchen, The After-Death History of My Mother, Between Earth and Sky, Endless Staircase, Earth Works, Which Way to the Egress?* and *Firing Back*. His writing has been published in *The New York Times, Newsday, The Nation,* and the *Wall Street Journal*.

Sophie Helene Menin writes about food and travel for numerous publications, including *The New York Times, Saveur* and *Departures*. She has an MA in Cultural Reporting and Criticism from NYU and a degree in Culinary Arts from The Institute of Culinary Education. She is currently working on a novel about food in America.

Donald Newlove's latest novel *Blindfolded Before the Firing Squad, or The Brothers Kirkmaus* will be published by Black Heron Press in 2007. He has just completed *Passion: Ardor and Desire in Great Writing*, the cap to his Handbook of the Soul series for writers and readers begun with *First Paragraphs, Painted Paragraphs* and *Invented Voices*. He is perhaps best-known for his memoir *Those Drinking Days: Myself and Other Writers*. He believes no risotto can have too much *parmigiano-reggiano*.

Lawrence F. O'Brien teaches English at Western New England College in Springfield, MA and edits the Connecticut poetry journal, *Common Ground*. His poetry has appeared in *Peregrine, Comstock Review, MacGuffin*, and other journals.

Michael Onofrey grew up in Los Angeles, but now lives in Japan, where he teaches English as a Second Language. His fiction has appeared in *Bryant Literary Review, Desert Voices, Lynx Eye, Nagoya Writes, Oyez Review, Pacific Coast Journal*, as well as in other literary journals and magazines.

Susie Paul teaches writing and literature at Auburn University, Montgomery. Her poems have appeared in numerous magazines and journals, including *The Georgia Review, Kalliope*, and *Negative Capability*. Frugality with style and a sense of abundance is a powerful theme in her family's character.

Peter Selgin's stories have appeared or are forthcoming in *Glimmer Train, Missouri Review, Antietam Review, The Literary Review, Bellevue Literary Review, The Sun, South Dakota Review, North Dakota Quarterly, Rattapallax, Salon.com*, the *Chicago Sun-Times, Alaska Quarterly Review*, and other magazines. His novel, *Life Goes to the Movies*, was a finalist for the James Jones First Novel Fellowship, and his short story collection, *nothing but water*, was short listed for the Iowa Fiction Award. His children's book, *S.S. Gigantic Across the Atlantic*, was a Scholastic Book Club selection and won the *Lemme Award* for best children's book, 2000.

Barbara Cunliffe Singleton has taught English to international students and has tasted yogurt in the US, South America, Tunisia, Turkey, Indonesia and Taiwan. Her articles have appeared in *Boston Review, Christian Science Monitor, India Currents, International Quarterly, International Social Work, The New York Times, Yuan Yang: A Journal of Hong Kong and International Writing*, and others.

C. Kevin Smith is a writer living in Big Sur, California. His fiction has won awards from the John Templeton Foundation and the Arch and Bruce Brown Foundation. He has contributed essays and reviews to the *Monterey County Weekly* and the *Lambda Book Report*, among other publications. Visit www.ckevinsmith.com.

Sue Taylor received an MFA in creative writing from the University of Minnesota in 2001. She lives in south Minneapolis with a domestic accomplice, an unruly child, some cats who are even worse, and a well-meaning but kind of stupid dog. She teaches English at Century Community College and she loves food in both fiction and real life.

Kerry Trautman lives in Findlay, Ohio with her husband and three children. Her poetry and short fiction have appeared in *The Glass Review, Fuel, Amelia, Poetry Letter*; on the web in *Logic Alley*; and in the anthology, *Tuesday Nights at Sam and Andy's Uptown Café* (Westron Press, 2001).

Will Walker lives in San Francisco with his wife and two dogs. He is a former editor of *The Haight Ashbury Literary Journal*. His work has appeared in *Bark* and *Provincetown Arts*, among other places. While he eats frequently, he has rarely written about food.

Anthony Russell White lives on a mountaintop in San Rafael, CA, and serves on the staff of the Nine Gates Mystery School. A poetic high point was a visit to the tomb of Jelaluddin Rumi at Konya, Turkey; he is still awed by Rumi's poetry. William Stafford has been another major influence.

Gary J. Whitehead's first full-length collection, *The Velocity of Dust*, was published by Salmon Publishing/Dufour Editions in 2004. His previous two chapbooks have won national awards. He's the recipient of a NYFA Fellowship in Poetry, the Pearl Hogrefe Fellowship in Creative Writing at Iowa State University, and PEN Northwest's Margery Davis Boyden Wilderness Writing Residency. Gary is a high school English teacher in Tenafly, New Jersey.

Angus Woodward lives, eats, and dines in Baton Rouge. His fiction and poetry have appeared in various journals, including *Bellingham Review, Laurel Review, Louisiana Literature, Rhino, Talking River Review, Xavier Review*, and in the anthology *Miniscule Fictions*.

Amy's Bread

We specialize in handmade, traditional BREADS.

More than bread...

We feature morning pastries, sandwiches, salads, cookies, bars, old-fashioned layer cakes and espresso beverages in our three bakery cafés.

Hell's Kitchen	672 Ninth Ave. NYC	212-977-2670
Chelsea Market	75 Ninth Ave. NYC	212-462-4338
The Village	250 Bleecker St. NYC	212-675-7802

www.amysbread.com

GET INSIDE THE KITCHENS – AND THE HEADS – OF SOME OF THE WORLD'S BEST CHEFS.

Start your collection today.
Get inspired.
Get Art Culinaire.

To subscribe, call 1-800-SO-TASTY, or visit us at www.getartc.com.

cimarron review

Subscription Rates
$24 per year ($28 outside USA)
$48 for two years ($55 outside USA)
$65 for three years ($72 outside USA)
Single Issues: $7.00 ($10.00 outside USA)

Submission Guidelines
Accepts submissions year round in Poetry, Fiction, and Non-Fiction
Simultaneous Submissions Welcome

205 Morrill Hall • Oklahoma State University • Stillwater, OK 74078
cimarronreview@yahoo.com • http://cimarronreview.okstate.edu

Gustiamo.com—Italy's Best Foods—is the ultimate source for authentic artisanal food from all regions of Italy

gustiamo.com

Italy's Best Foods

A passion for forgotten tastes and wholesome ingredients leads Gustiamo's search for indigenous Italian flavors: from **Mediterranean Bluefin tuna** fished in the pristine waters off the island of Favignana in Sicily to the **highest percentage San Marzano gene tomatoes** grown naturally on Mount Vesuvius, from **extra virgin olive oils** produced by small estates with control of all the steps of production "in house" and **gianduja chocolates** traditionally made in Piemonte with Tonda Gentile variety hazelnuts to **slow dried artisanal pasta** from the Latini farm where passionate experiments with disappearing wheat varieties have produced masterpieces. Log on to www.gustiamo.com to find pure Italian foods.

As a reader of *Alimentum*, receive a 10% discount on your order placed with Gustiamo.com. Just write "Alimentum" on the "special shipping/delivery instructions" field at the bottom of the shopping cart. Offer valid until October 31, 2006.

www.gustiamo.com • 718-860-2949 • gethelp@gustiamo.com

From the *New York Times* bestselling author of *Cod* and *Salt*

The Big Oyster

MARK KURLANSKY

The Big Oyster
History on the Half Shell

"**This is fascinating stuff.**"—*The Wall Street Journal*

"The story of a city that loved the oyster not wisely but too well. . . . Part treatise, part miscellany, **unfailingly entertaining.**"
—William Grimes, *The New York Times*

"**A fascinating history** of the mollusk's role in N.Y.C.'s development."—*People*

A Ballantine Hardcover | www.ballantinebooks.com

The Sub-Zero & Wolf Showroom

THERE ARE ART GALLERIES LESS INSPIRING.

Architect: Peter Tow
Photographer: James Wilkins

Where else can you walk among great works of art — even masterpieces — and touch everything in sight? Behold your local Sub-Zero and Wolf Showroom. Here, you can see, tinker, and get inspired. Well-informed (but never stuffy) consultants are here to answer every question, take you through actual kitchen installations and product demonstrations, and, if you want, refer you to the Sub-Zero and Wolf dealer nearest you. Call for showroom hours and the next product demonstration.

goldman
ASSOCIATES
www.gany.com

SUB-ZERO

WOLF

VISIT YOUR REGIONAL SHOWROOM.

Roslyn Heights, NY	Manhattan, NY	Pine Brook, NJ	Short Hills, NJ
2 Lambert Street	150 E. 58th Street	25 Riverside Drive	The Mall at Short Hills
516-484-7800	8th Floor	973-882-9400	1200 Morris Tpke.
	212-207-9223		973-376-9090